Praise for *The Power of TED**

"It's no exaggeration to say that our world would be a better place if everyone read it."

　　—**Lisa Lahey**, Ed.D., Harvard Graduate School of Education; co-author of *Immunity to Change* and *An Everyone Culture*

"When practical advice meets profound, yet simple, explanations for human behavior, we can learn, change, and grow."

　　—**Annie McKee**, co-author of *Becoming a Resonant Leader*, *Resonant Leadership*, and *Primal Leadership*

"This powerful little book points the way toward a hugely fulfilling life of empowering relationships—at work, at home, in the whole of your life."

　　—**Gay Hendricks**, Ph.D. ,and **Kathlyn Hendricks**, Ph.D., authors of *Conscious Loving*

"Knowing the characteristics of the Dreaded Drama Triangle (DDT) and its creative alternative, TED* (*The Empowerment Dynamic) is remarkably transformative. It's impossible to overstate my enthusiasm for this book!"

　　—**Brian Johnson**, Founder, PhilosophersNotes

"TED* is utterly simple and endlessly nuanced."

　　—**Molly Gordon**, MCC, Shaboom, Inc.

"Beautiful, deep, friendly, and fun! This masterful story hits the sweet spot where spirituality and practicality meet. TED* provides essential wisdom for anyone committed to living a purposeful and passionate life."

　　—**Eric Klein**, author of *To Do or Not*

D0181043

"Simple, beautiful, life-changing. You'll want to share a copy with everyone you know!"

> —**Jane Nelsen**, Ed.D., author of *From Here to Serenity: Reconnecting to Your Heart and Soul* and the *Positive Discipline* series

"Like all the best personal growth books, *The Power of TED** doesn't stop at providing a clear path toward greater well-being. David Emerald's life-changing story actually creates a positive shift in your thinking. Reading *TED** is like having a private session with a gifted spiritual teacher and coach: as you make this delightful journey, you awaken to powerful new possibilities."

> —**Jennifer Louden**, author of *Comfort Secrets of Busy Women* and the *Comfort Book* series

"With this lighthearted yet deceptively simple fable, David Emerald has given us . . . remarkably rich insights that enable us to break old patterns and replace them with more fruitful ways of knowing ourselves and others. A unique and most practical addition to any mentor's or coach's toolbox."

> —**Laurent A. Parks-Daloz**, author of *Mentor: Guiding the Journey of Adult Learners* and co-author of *Common Fire: Leading Lives of Commitment in a Complex World*

"*The Power of TED** provided more insight into interpersonal relationships and the potential dysfunction of human relationships than did my psychiatry rotation and years of experience working in a public hospital."

> —**Kenneth K. Adams,** MD

"TED* has increased my awareness; with greater awareness, I see a fuller picture and am able to make better decisions."

> —**Randy Eisenman,** Managing Partner, Satori Capital

"*The Power of TED** is a simple, nonjudgmental message of hope. This book sets the stage for people with diverse interests and viewpoints to work together in innovative ways to address root causes rather than merely symptoms."

　　—**Deborah Nankivell**, Chief Executive Officer, Fresno Business Council

"*The Power of TED** has been deeply rewarding for myself and 1st Global. Being aware of the role I am playing and the choices I make has rendered meaningful change in my life. TED* has also been a key factor in helping 1st Global deliver on its purpose—to enable intentional living."

　　—**David C. Knoch**, President of 1st Global

"Inspiring, grounded, and accessible all describe the powerful presence of David Emerald's *The Power of TED* (*The Empowerment Dynamic)*! This book and body of work is one of the best frameworks I have ever seen for understanding the human experience from a spiritual perspective. Both during our Sunday services and the seminar that followed, David touched the minds, hearts, and souls that heard his wisdom and explored the way to move from Victim to Creator in their lives."

　　—**Debra Carter Williams**, former Senior Minister, Unity of Naples
　　Church (Florida)

"What a pleasure it was to start reading this easy to read, 'can't put it down until you finish it' book containing practical suggestions to improve the quality of life. Whether you manage a department or a family, or you live alone, this dynamic paperback is no ordinary day at the beach. . . . It's a journey that will touch and transform every part of the reader's life."

　　—**Patrick Cooney**, SPHR, Human Resources Director, City of West Palm
　　Beach (Florida)

"David Emerald has written a beautiful and thoughtful book that gives us a useful tool for living empowered lives."

> —**Merlene Miller**, author of *Staying Clean and Sober: Complementary and Natural Strategies for Healing the Addicted Brain* and *Reversing the Regression Spiral* (and others)

"Profoundly simple . . . not necessarily easy . . . yet, imminently possible for each of us to live as the Creator we are. David Emerald reveals a practical key and depth of understanding that will change your life—a powerful book. I hope everyone has a chance to receive the power of TED*!"

> —**Dorothy J. Maver**, Ph.D., Project Director, Kosmos Associates

"Eloquent in delivering its simple yet profound message. I've already given a copy to my wife, my father, and two business associates!"

> —**Tommy Glenn,** Entrepreneur and Former President, Netbank Payment Systems

"Whether we are helping professionals, corporate managers, leaders, or parents—anyone in relationship—I see enormous opportunities for resisting our old tendencies to play the victim . . . TED* is a wake-up call to these behavior habits and what they cost us in the quality of our lives. And TED* shows how to make more empowering choices. . . . If you are a human being, read this book!"

> —**Fran Fisher,** MCC, Founder and Former Owner, Academy for Coach Training and Living Your Vision®

"*The Power of TED** is the power of Tao. It identifies an empowerment dialectic that rings true and resonates with common sense and practicality. I not only find immediate usage with my individual clients, but find it valuably applicable to larger scale consulting engagements as well."

> —**Bert Parlee**, Integral Coach, Advisor, and Psychologist, and Ken Wilber's former "Chief of Staff" at the Integral Institute, Boulder, CO

THE POWER OF TED*

*THE EMPOWERMENT DYNAMIC

David Emerald

THE POWER OF TED*
*THE EMPOWERMENT DYNAMIC

Published by

POLARIS

Polaris Publishing
321 High School Rd NE – PMB 295
Bainbridge Island, WA 98110

THIRD EDITION

Cover and Interior Design by Robert Lanphear
Illustrations by Obadinah

ISBN 978-0-9968718-0-8

SEL031000 SELF-HELP / Personal Growth / General
PSY017000 PSYCHOLOGY / Interpersonal Relations
SEL044000 SELF-HELP / Self-Management / General

Printed in the United States of America

To all the

Challengers, Coaches, and Co-Creators

in my life

Contents

FOREWORD

BY LISA LAHEY

Tell me, what is it you plan to do with your one wild and precious life?

—Mary Oliver

I've shared Oliver's line with many people over the years. When I do, three observations emerge:

1) People agree on one point: each of us has one life.

2) People tend to respond positively or negatively to the quotation; few people respond neutrally.

3) Within those two reactions, there is significant variation in why people feel as they do.

Some people are delighted by the question's reminder that their lives are in their own hands, while for others, it is a novel but wonderful idea that they could actually plan to do something with their lives. Other people feel ashamed of not being able to answer the question, and others are angry with the presumption that they can plan their lives. Still others laugh at the word "precious," feeling quite clear that there is nothing precious about their lives at the moment. Instead, life feels like a weight, a fight, or worse.

Some feel so beaten down that they say it seems foolhardy to even imagine being in charge of their own lives. You may have had another reaction.

I've come to see people's responses to these sixteen simple words as a window into two essential ways we see ourselves and our lives. Broadly speaking, one way is to see ourselves at the mercy of those around us, and the other is to see ourselves as having agency over our lives. We can move back and forth between these two mindsets, though people seem to operate predominantly from one or the other.

As if it wasn't enough of a burden to experience oneself at the mercy of others, I've noticed that many people who feel this way are also suffering, feeling stuck, thinking badly of themselves (often quietly— though some people cover that up with their anger), and are almost always on their own, by themselves. They find it hard to ask for help for many different reasons, including not admitting to themselves that they need help and not wanting to appear weak by asking for help.

Asking for help is hard. After all, we live in a culture in which the tacit message is that we "ought" to be able to handle such challenges ourselves. This notion is mistaken.

As a developmental psychologist, I can tell you that our individual development needs to be nurtured, and that an ideal environment is one that both supports and challenges us. Too often, we go without both of these conditions.

If I could wave the proverbial magic wand on behalf of each of us becoming our best selves, I would make it so we could ask for help and we could do so before things go terribly wrong, or before we feel overwhelmed and excessively stressed from being in over our heads. Without someone else's perspective, we tend to go around and around, repeating our default patterns and getting nowhere (except perhaps to feeling worse about ourselves for our lack of progress).

Help is here, in this gem of a book. In this short, fast-paced and wisdom-packed parable, Emerald takes us by the hand and lovingly shows us how our psychological default is to operate unconsciously from a state of fear and to take on different drama based roles as a result. He helps us to see how living out of fear not only keeps us small but creates a dynamic in which we keep others small as well. In other words, we limit our own potential as well as the people around us. We lose a connection to our vision and purpose. Emerald helps us understand the variation of people's responses I've described here, and how any of us can move from believing and reinforcing the belief that we have no agency in our lives to a belief that we are the only ones who are in charge of our lives.

Because this is counter-cultural, I want to repeat that developing our capacity to take responsibility for our lives is an achievement that needs to be cultivated. If we did so, we would be able to use our one wild and precious life to create something meaningful. We would be available to support other people to do the same. And together, we might intentionally participate in our communities (in our home, our work, our neighborhoods) to do something bigger than any of us individually could. Dare I say that we could together create peace?

If all this sounds lofty and impossible, let me say it this way: If we could develop our capacity to plan and live our lives fully, we would feel less like victims, helpless to solve the problems other people make for us. We would no longer feel so exhausted from fighting, feeling badly about ourselves for not fighting back, or for believing that we are not good enough. We would have energy to create more of the life we want.

So read this book. Let Emerald take you by the hand. Remind yourself that he has walked this very path (as have I). And go find the community, even if it is just one other person, to provide you with what you want, need, and deserve.

> *When it's over, I want to say: all my life I was a bride married to amazement. I was the bridegroom, taking the world into my arms.*
>
> —Mary Oliver

Lisa Lahey Ed.D., Cambridge, MA
Harvard Graduate School of Education
Minds at Work

NEW PREFACE
FOR THE 10TH ANNIVERSARY EDITION

"This book changes lives."

That message has been communicated countless times over the past decade through emails, during workshops, at speaking events, in on-line book reviews, and in casual encounters when people learn that I am the author of TED*.

And countless times I have been left almost speechless. I will share the reason why in a minute.

From all reports, TED* has impacted marriages, improved relationships between parents and children, informed pre-marital counseling, and healed multi-generational family drama. It's been used in middle school and high school curricula, in college social work and psychology classes, in addiction treatment programs and groups, in diabetes education and other chronic health challenge situations, in community poverty outreach and training programs, and in church youth and book study groups. It's been beneficial for the community of Rwandan immigrants who fled to the United States after their country's 1994 genocide and their work of reconciliation between Hutus and Tutsis. TED* has been widely deployed in leadership academies, by leadership teams in organizations, and has become the cornerstone of company cultures.

And these are only examples that have been brought to our attention. There are others we do not know of.

Here's one illustration. A gentleman who looked to be in his early 40s stopped by our book table at a recent conference. "I have been looking forward to meeting and thanking you for writing this book—it saved my marriage." He proceeded to tell me a story of sitting in a hotel room in his home town, estranged from his wife, holding a book a friend had given him, recommending he read it that night. He laid down on the bed, he said, and didn't get up until he was done reading *The Power of TED**. The next day he called his wife, apologized for his part in the drama of their marriage, and said he wanted to create a new relationship.

I didn't know what to say or do, so I did and said what I have so many times: I stood, shook his hand, put my hand on my heart and said, "Thank you, I am so grateful that TED* has touched your life."

Beyond that, I am nearly speechless in such encounters because I often don't feel worthy of the praise simply because, like everyone else, on a daily basis I, too, am seeking to live the principles and practices contained in this story of David and Ted and Sophia walking and talking along the shore where surf meets sand—and where the human experience meets our spiritual essence.

You see, the ways of thinking, relating, and taking action contained in this book changed my life as well—and continue to. For me the old adage is true: we teach what we most need to learn.

The Story Behind the Story

The time has come to share a little of the genesis of what eventually became *The Power of TED**.

At a critical time in my life, I faced all of the realities that the character David faces in the story. While working with a psychotherapist (a healthy choice when facing such challenges in life), I learned about the Karpman Drama Triangle and its roles of Victim, Persecutor, and Rescuer.

Then, one fateful morning, as I was sitting engaged in my morning "quiet time" ritual—a practice of some combination of inspirational readings, prayer, silence, and contemplation—a moment of surrender surfaced and silently I said to the God of my understanding, "I am ready to relinquish my Victim stance in the world, but I need to know what is the opposite of Victim?" Immediately the word "Creator" came into my awareness. While I did not actually "hear" a voice, I can understand how some could say they do. My eyes flew open and I drew a deep breath. It was an utterly unexpected personal epiphany.

That morning began the journey that eventually led to TED*.

Looking back, many seemingly miraculous meetings and events took place—too many to detail here. I can attest to the famous observation made by W. H. Murray (The Scottish Himalayan Expedition [1951]:

"The moment one definitely commits oneself, then Providence moves too. All sorts of things occur to help one that would never otherwise have occurred. A whole stream of events issues from the decision which no one could have dreamed would have come their way."

Among them, for me, was learning of the work of Robert Fritz shortly after my morning epiphany and engaging in his "Technologies for Creating"; and then, not long after, meeting Bob Anderson, my dear friend and col-league for now over a quarter-century who, through our shared passion for leadership development, introduced me to the mindsets and models of the Orientations contained in the story; and over a dozen years ago meeting Donna Zajonc, my wife, business partner, and the "Mom" of TED* who first encouraged me to take that personal epiphany and begin to share it with others.

Given my more than three decades of community and organizational communication, leadership and organization development, it would have been easy to write a more traditional, nonfiction leadership book. (And for those for whom such an approach might be more appealing, I suggest your start with the Appendix, which contains a narrative outline of the concepts contained in the story.)

Instead, the spirit of TED* intervened. The Call was to write a fable about Self Leadership. For this is what I have come to learn, a lesson I am reminded of almost daily: the way we lead our own lives has everything to do with the quality of leadership we bring to our most important relationships, our families, our organizations, our communities, and—now, more than ever—our world.

As I write, our human family seems to be careening toward the ultimate choice point: will we continue the downward spiral of fear, reactivity, and drama or stop, pause, and choose to upgrade our way of being in relationship with one another as Creators capable of honoring and respecting our essential unity with all its splendid diversity?

It starts with me and you and how we lead our own lives. My prayer is that TED* touches and enriches your own life so that, in turn, you can help others.

David Emerald

CHAPTER 1

A FATEFUL MEETING

From the bench where I sat overlooking the beach, it seemed I could see forever. The ocean spread out in a blue expanse, undulating its way into infinity. Yet I couldn't really enjoy it. Inside I was constricted. The surf, some hundred feet below the bluff on which my bench sat, normally would have sounded soothing. Its calm was lost on me as I struggled with an insistent emptiness inside.

It had been a particularly painful period. The bloom was, indeed, off the rose. A couple of years ago, my wife and I had bought the perfect suburban starter home, nothing lacking but the white picket fence. We had envisioned it as the place to start our family; for so long

1

we had dreamed about having children. Then, months after the untimely death of my dad, with whom I had been very close, we received word from our doctor that I was infertile. Not only had I lost Dad, but now I felt that I was the victim of my biology. To my mind, the link between generations—first between me and my dad, and now between me and the child I had dreamed of fathering—was permanently shattered.

After months of anguishing over options, my wife entered her grief and withdrew from our fragile marriage, unwilling to consider adoption or medical alternatives. Feeling abandoned and alone, I descended into despair as we separated and, eventually, divorced. I was bereft.

Everywhere I looked, my life hurt. Tears filled my eyes and the beauty of the beach before me became even more obscured. I had always assumed I would have a family when the time was right, and that the marriage vows of "in good times and bad" would see us through any trials and tribulations. Not so. The time, it seemed, was never, and the vow proved to be conditional. I lived a good moral and ethical life. The questions swirled and tumbled through my mind: "What sort of karma is this? What seeds have I sown to reap this unjust penalty? Why me?" The void felt as big as the sea before me.

I took my pen from the clasp of my leather-bound journal and opened it to a new page. This repository of my thoughts and questions and yearnings had been a constant companion over the years. Journaling had become a way of processing my experiences, and I was grateful for the insights that often emerged.

As I wrote, emotions washed over me and my rational mind found its still, small voice. Instead of answering my questions, it simply whispered that this was the hand I had been dealt. Life was challenging me to find a way through what seemed to be a life of powerlessness and victimization.

In this struggle between heart and head, inwardly I cried out to Spirit, "I'm sick and tired of feeling so small!" And in that moment, I chose to surrender my stance as Victim. But for the life of me, I didn't know what to re-place it with. "What," I wrote, "is the opposite of Victim?" If the crashing waves contained the answer, I didn't understand their language.

In that moment I closed the journal and returned the pen to the holder that served as a clasp. Closing my eyes, I breathed deeply, savoring the salt air. Again I inquired, "What is the opposite of Victim?" This time the response was immediate: "Creator," the inner voice announced.

"The opposite of Victim is Creator."

I felt a chill course up my spine, and I took a deep, full breath of sea air. Suddenly there emerged a feeling I had not had in a very long time. A fresh sense of hope began to make itself known. I sat for a few precious moments drinking in the sounds of the surf and the release that accompanied the revelation of this new and different way of being in the world.

I wondered, "What does it mean to know that the opposite of Victim is Creator? What do I do now?" I knew I had to stay open and receptive to whatever guidance might be forthcoming.

A New Friend

I don't know how many minutes I sat there, enveloped by the sounds and the scents of the sea, before I heard the faint sound of footsteps on the sandy path leading up to the bench.

When I opened my eyes again, I saw that someone had silently joined me on my seaside bench. He sighed, "What a sight. It's hard not to be inspired from this vantage point, wouldn't you say?" All I could do was nod. I managed a slight smile.

"Hi, I'm Ted," he said, extending his hand. "Mind if I sit here? I don't mean to intrude."

I shook his firm, friendly, and strangely familiar hand. "David," I simply said.

I had come to that bluff overlooking the sea to contemplate, to try to make some sense out of the unexpected twists and turns my life had taken. It seemed that a new choice was being offered me, though I was anything but clear about what it all meant. My emotions were caught in a crosscurrent between grief and hope. Despite the new direction I had been given from within, I felt disoriented.

And now here was this friendly stranger beside me. He had a walking stick—more like a staff—that he held with both hands between his knees. I couldn't tell if it was fashioned from the branch of a tree or if it had been a long piece of driftwood that may have washed up on the beach. In any case, it was worn smooth except for a few knots that appeared like dark eyes along the shaft.

We sat there in silence for a long time. I didn't know it yet, but I had just met a teacher who would help me answer some of the most important questions in my life. It was the beginning of getting to know Ted.

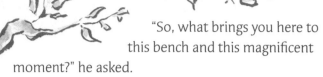

"So, what brings you here to this bench and this magnificent moment?" he asked.

A fair question, I thought. But who was this guy? Why should I tell a stranger what was going on with me? There was a quiet expectancy in his presence, as if he knew I had something to share. Yet there was a spaciousness that put no pressure on me to speak right away. I sensed that I could wait five seconds, five minutes, or five hours. Time was not of the essence—what was on my mind and heart was. There was a comfort I felt. He seemed so friendly and his question was certainly an open invitation.

I ventured forth, "Oh, I've come here to think. You know, just to sit and reflect."

"That's good to do from time to time. It's all too easy to run through life without reflecting. Life's lessons can be lost if you never pause. What a beautiful place to come and take stock."

"Yes, it is," I replied, "though I have to admit I sometimes lose sight of all this beauty when I get caught up in my own drama."

"Oh yes, drama," Ted remarked. "That seems to be such a big part of the human experience. Look at all these people walking on the beach. Every one of them probably has some sort of drama going on in their lives. They all have their stories. What, if I may ask, is yours? I don't mean to intrude. I'm just curious."

Then it all spilled out. I told him about everything: my recent divorce, the death of my dad. I even told him about my infertility. He nodded, encouraging me. I didn't detect even an ounce of judgment coming from Ted—or pity, for that matter. He looked out over the ocean, turning my way occasionally and nodding in acknowledgment. Emboldened by his calm acceptance, I shared the full depth of my inner struggle, how I had felt like a victim. The whole mess just flowed out, as Ted listened. For some reason, though, I wasn't quite ready yet to divulge the revelation that Creator was my new alternative, the stance I must take to replace the old sense of being a victim of my own life. Instead I said, "I've come to see how much of my life I have lived from the perspective of being a victim. I'm ready for something else."

Ready for BFOs

"You're not alone, you know," said Ted. "Victimhood is the malaise of humanity. It is everywhere, in every language. Most news reports are stories of Victims and Persecutors and, sometimes, Rescuers. People look for someone to blame. Sometimes they demand compensation for their victimization; sometimes they strike back. Terrorists attack and leave victims in their wake, all the while describing themselves as victims of oppression. On the roadways, some drivers feel so victimized by the chaos of traffic that they're filled with rage and lash out. People talk about being victims of abuse and neglect, victims of alcoholic or drug-addicted parents, even victims of birth order among siblings. At work, people talk about their victimization at the hands of an insensitive boss, a backstabbing coworker, or the company they work for. Some people feel constantly victimized by that elusive goblin they call 'the system.'"

I let his words sink in. As I thought about how often I gave voice to my own sense of victimhood, I offered, "It's amazing, isn't it, how often we use the blaming words of victimization: The traffic made me late. I got up on the wrong side of the bed. I ended up in the wrong lane at the grocery store. The examples are end-less. There must be a better way."

Ted turned and put his hand on my shoulder. "It's true, there is."

I asked him, "But who are you, anyway? What brings *you* to this spot overlooking the beach?"

Ted wrapped his hands around his staff and looked out at the scene before us. "I come here a lot, to take in the ocean and to do the kind of contempla-tion that just naturally arises in this beautiful place. Today I saw you here, so I came over to sit and share a few thoughts."

"Thoughts about what?"

"About the very subject you've introduced—about being a Victim and the desire for a different way of being in the world. I've learned a few things that I think you may find useful, things that may surprise you."

"Well, if you know something that I don't, I mean about not being a Victim, well, then I'm all ears," I said.

"Good," said Ted. "You need to know, however, that what I have to say could make you a little uncomfort-able. That's because what I say will probably challenge the ways you engage with just about every area of your life. Your relationships. Your work. The way you deal with disappointments. Everything. Are you up for that?"

I looked out at the waves rising and rolling into the shore. Why had this spirited stranger suddenly shown up by my side? The encounter had a dreamlike quality. I wasn't sure what to say. I could have got up and walked away, but I didn't want to. Somehow I felt entirely at ease with Ted. And I was intrigued.

Ted continued, "If this sounds interesting to you and you want to hear more, then it's only fair to warn you: Be prepared to be visited by BFOs."

I chuckled and turned to him. "I'm going to be visited by UFOs?"

"No . . . BFOs. A BFO is a Blinding Flash of the Obvious. It's something you already know but which lies just beyond the edge of your conscious awareness. When they come, welcome them. A BFO is a very positive sign. It means that you're awakening to new ways of thinking and being."

"Oh, good. For a minute there I thought you were about to tell me that you were from outer space," I laughed.

"If anything, I'm from inner space!"

"Who *are* you, then?" I said.

"Just a friend, bringing you a lighthearted approach to a most serious subject: how you relate to your life experiences. You could say I'm a countercultural type. I live in the world in my own way. So many people meet their life experience from the Victim Orientation—just as you've begun to notice for yourself. I have a different orientation. It's a simple way of being, though it's not always easy.

"I guess I'm also a revolutionary—or, rather, an evolutionary! As an evolutionary facilitator, I'd like to offer you another way to live—if you choose it. At the end of the day, what you do will always be your choice. No one can ever take that away from you. In fact, it's why you're here: to make the choices that create your life."

It was a lot to take in. I searched his face. He didn't look like a fanatic. In fact, the gentleness in his eyes made me feel relaxed in spite of all my recent turmoil He added, "I won't mind if you'd rather not do this right now, you know. It's entirely up to you. In the end, it's all about choice."

My choice. I sat another moment in silence as Ted waited patiently. Should I leave, or stay and see where this weird conversation might go? I decided I had nothing to lose. And anyway, listening to Ted was already a lot more interesting than wallowing in the worries that had brought me up here in the first place.

"Would you like to walk with me for awhile, down on the beach?" asked Ted.

"Okay, sure."

Ted and I got up together and started down the meandering path to the shore. Little did I know that I was setting out on the path to a whole new way of seeing.

CHAPTER 2

THE DREADED DRAMA TRIANGLE

We walked down the slope of the bluff onto a path that wound its way to the sandy shore below.

"So, David, tell me more about your thoughts on victimhood," Ted suggested.

"Well," I said, "it seems like victimhood is all-pervasive. I've been thinking about it since I learned about the Drama Triangle. Ever heard of it?"

"Tell me more."

"It comes from the work of Stephen Karpman, a psychotherapist who described the Triangle in the late 1960s. It involves three roles, all of which I play pretty well."

"Yes," said Ted, "it's been around a while, all right. That model has helped countless people make

13

sense of their situations. What strikes you about it?"

I told Ted what I had learned about the Drama Triangle. "The central role is **Victim**, when I feel as if other people or situations are acting upon me, and I can't do anything about it. Sometimes it feels like being attacked, and sometimes it's just a hardship. I might feel mistreated or discounted, and maybe out of control.

"The second role is **Persecutor** or perpetrator in situations of abuse. The Persecutor is the perceived cause of the Victim's woes.

"The third role is **Rescuer**, the one who intervenes on behalf of the victim, to deliver the victim from harm by the Persecutor."

Just then, Ted and I rounded a bend into a jagged maze of sandstone blocking the path to the beach. As I stepped out of the rocks and onto the sandy path, my foot gave way. Whomp! I landed squarely on my rear. We laughed (nothing was hurt but my pride), and Ted offered his hand. "Here let me help," he said, pulling me upright. I spanked the sand off the seat of my pants, and we continued gingerly down the path.

"That was an interesting example of what you just described."

"How's that?" I asked.

"Did you feel like a Victim when you fell back there?" Ted asked.

"I guess so, in a way."

"So, if you were the Victim, who was the Persecutor?"

"You were in front of me, so I know you didn't push me," I chuckled. "So I'm not sure there *was* a Persecutor."

"Every Victim requires a Persecutor," Ted explained. "But the Persecutor isn't always necessarily a person. The Persecutor could also be a condition or a circumstance. A persecuting condition might be a disease, such as cancer or a heart attack or an injury. A persecuting circumstance could be a natural disaster, like a hurricane or an earthquake or a house burning down. So, what was the Persecutor in your situation just now?"

I thought for a moment. "The loose sand, maybe, or my shoes," I observed.

"Right," said Ted. "Either of those could be identified as Persecutor. And I was the Rescuer when I reached down to help you up. It's a simple example and there was no real harm done in this situation, but you just saw all three parts of the Drama Triangle in action.

"Other people encounter much more intense versions of the Drama Triangle every day," he continued.

"Whether it is subtle or intense, the effort to observe and understand this pattern is the first step in breaking the cycle of Victimhood."

We paused to survey the length of the shore. Seagulls called out as they glided along the surf line. The waves roared, as a fine mist swept over us. I breathed deeply.

"Let's walk a little closer to the water. I want to show you something." Ted moved with ease. His gait was relaxed as he matched his pace to mine. As we walked, he glanced down at the shells and bits of driftwood marking the sand. Ted bent down, picked up a seashell, and began tracing a large triangle in the moist, hard-packed sand.

VICTIMHOOD, THE DEATH OF A DREAM

"Here's the Drama Triangle you were talking about," said Ted. "It's great that you know about these three roles. Let's look at the dynamics that take place between them."

"Here's the Victim." He scratched the letter *V* in the sand.

"Victims may be defensive, submissive, over-accommodating to others, passive-aggressive in

conflict, dependent
on others for self-
worth, overly sensitive,
even manipulative. They're often
angry, resentful, and envious, feeling
unworthy or ashamed about their circumstances. Have you ever felt or acted this way?"

I remembered the months before my wife and I had
separated, how I had alternated between walking on
eggshells and blaming her—often loudly—for the distance growing between us. I loathed my fearful pattern
in romantic relationships: an unspoken agreement to be
whoever my partner wanted, resentfully avoiding her
abandonment.

"These roles describe attitudes I usually associate with
other people," I said, "but I see how I've acted in some of
the same ways myself."

Ted nodded. "There's another characteristic at the
very heart of Victimhood. At the core of any Victim,
you'll find the psychic death of a dream. All Victims
have experienced a loss—a thwarted desire or aspiration—even if they're not aware of it. It might be a loss of
freedom or health or a sense of safety. The loss might
even be one of identity or of a 'reality,' such as when a

belief (my spouse is faithful) is shattered (my spouse has had an affair)."

That was certainly true for me. My dream of a family had died when I learned of my infertility. My belief in a wife staying by my side no matter what wilted with my divorce. And my identity as a son seemed to have died right along with Dad.

Ted continued, "The Victim feels out of control, believing life can't change for the better. Taking that position, one feels powerless, helpless, hopeless, and at the mercy of unseen forces. The Victim reacts with depression or shame. You feel sorry for yourself."

"I can't tell you how many times I've privately thought, 'Poor Me!'"

Ted smiled calmly and gazed out at the surf. "'Poor Me' is the Victim's identity. That way of seeing yourself and your life experience determines how you relate to the world around you. Your orientation defines your reality. There's actually a lot of ego involved in maintaining Victimhood."

"Wait a minute," I said, "are you saying being a victim is just a matter of seeing myself that way? What about a battered child or someone enslaved against their will? Are you implying they created their own victimization?"

"Not at all," Ted responded. "The experience of being the victim of violence is very real. There's no denying that people treat each other badly all over the world, every day. I'm saying one has a choice—however difficult or painful—about how to relate to those experiences. If you identify yourself as a Victim, your choices are limited. There's another way to see things which allows you to meet even the most difficult circumstances. But I'm getting ahead of myself. Before you see things another way, you must understand how Victimhood works.

"A while ago I met a young woman who told me her story.

"Her name was Sophia, and her marriage was a mess. Her husband, Dan, had confessed to having an affair. Sophia had tried everything to avoid this downward spiral, even canceling her dance class, thinking Dan might be happier if she spent more time at home. Things improved for a while, but soon Dan began working late several times a week.

"One night Sophia exploded. 'I gave up my class to be with you, and you're hardly ever home!'

"Dan argued, 'Even when I *am* home, you're doing work you bring home, or your nose is buried in a book! I can't get your attention!'

"The two decided to set aside Thursday as dinner-out-together night. After several months of special evenings, Dan and Sophia found less and less to talk about. Then one night, right there in the restaurant, Dan admitted his infidelity.

"Caught in public, Sophia felt she couldn't react. When I met her, she was trying to figure out how to win back Dan's heart from a faceless foe. She feared losing him and facing life alone."

Ted continued, "The feelings that Victims have, just as Sophia did, are all fear-based and produce various anxieties. These feelings, which often seesaw between passivity and aggression, drive behaviors. When human beings are afraid, they're programmed to react. This program—to fight, flee, or freeze—isn't all bad. It helps the species survive."

"I can remember times when I have reacted in all three of those ways," I offered. "Toward the end of my marriage I got defensive. I felt so guilty and ashamed about my infertility, and fought off those feelings by lashing out with biting comments. Or I just withdrew—a way of fleeing, I guess. Not sure what you mean about freezing, though."

"Imagine you're trying to start a car that's buried

under a snowdrift," Ted explained. "It doesn't budge.
You freeze if you stop and take no action, either toward
or away from the source of your fear. It's giving up
and giving in to hopelessness. Frozen in fear, you avoid
responsibility because you think your experience is
beyond your control. This stance keeps you from making decisions, solving problems, or going after what you
want in life.

"In the position of Victim you become hyper-vigilant,
always anticipating the next bout of suffering. All you
see in life are problems. And these problems, whether
they are people or circumstances, become your
Persecutors, the perpetrators of your misery. The Victim
role isn't maintained in a vacuum. Some person or thing
must wear the Persecutor label."

Ted walked around the triangle in the sand. I stood
with my hands in my pockets and looked out to sea. It
seemed there were as many faces of the Victim in this
world as there were waves in the ocean. Ted knelt down
and scrawled *P* for *Persecutor* by the next corner of the
triangle.

THE PERSECUTOR

Ted continued, "As you said, the Persecutor is the
perceived cause of the Victim's woes. Persecutors and

Victims are symbiotic; one can't exist without the other. According to the dictionary, persecute means 'to harass in a manner designed to injure, grieve, or afflict; or to annoy with persistent or urgent approaches (as attacks, pleas, or importunities).'

"Often the Persecutor is a person, but not always. As I said when you slipped on the path, persecution can be a condition, like a health challenge, or a circumstance, such as losing your home in a fire. But whether person, condition, or circumstance, the Persecutor gets the blame for causing the Victim's feelings of grief, despair, and hopelessness."

"Hmm, I can see all three kinds of Persecutors in my life. My wife seemed like my Persecutor when she became distant. My infertility was a persecuting condition, and Dad's death was a persecuting circumstance. No wonder I feel like a Victim."

Ted responded, "The Poor Me identity is reinforced by the Persecutor, who looks down on the Victim with an attitude of 'You poor so-and-so!'

"When the Persecutor is a condition or a circumstance, of course, there's no personalization. That doesn't mean you don't take it personally—you do. But conditions and circumstances don't have personalities, even if hurricanes do have names!"

Ted chuckled at himself, then cleared his throat and continued. "When the Persecutor is an actual person, the one who adopts that role tries to dominate others through blame, criticism, and/or oppression. These people are often authoritarian and rigid in their views, exerting power over others in an effort to keep others from having power over them. Persecutors may act grandiose and self-righteous to mask their own insecurity. They can be manipulative and defensive, often launching preemptive attacks. For Persecutors, all situations are win/lose. Their motto is 'Win at any cost!'"

"Persecutors sound really heavy-duty. They're fearless characters, aren't they?" I said.

"They may be heavy-handed in persecuting, but they're also subtle sometimes. I don't want to offend you, David, but if you think you've never been a Persecutor, think again. Remember what you said about vacillating between being passive and angry, blaming your former wife?"

"Sure, I remember." I felt uncomfortable as I sensed where Ted might be going.

"How do you think she saw you when you lashed out at her?" he asked.

"Well, probably like, um, a Persecutor?"

"Exactly. Victims often react to situations in ways that make them Persecutors in the eyes of others. That's important in the Drama Triangle. Persecutors, like Victims, act out of fear. They may seem fearless, but actually Persecutors are almost always former Victims. They're mobilized by the fear of becoming a Victim, nursing angry resentments about times when they felt victimized. Persecutors inwardly declare, 'I'll never be a Victim again!' Ultimately, what they fear most is loss of control."

I laughed. "Reminds me of Scarlett O'Hara in the movie *Gone with the Wind*. She proclaims, 'I will never go hungry again!' after she's lost her social position and all her possessions. She feels like a Victim, but she ends up being Rhett Butler's Persecutor."

Ted smiled. "It sounds like a good example, although I must admit that movies aside, there's enough drama for me in the everyday lives of the people I meet. A couple of weeks after I first met Sophia, she brought her partner, Dan, to meet me."

Dan felt bad that his affair had caused Sophia such pain. But, he added, it wasn't as if he had been planning it. He felt that in many ways Sophia was responsible. Dan wanted to be with someone who wanted to talk and laugh with him at the end of a hard day. He was pleasantly surprised when Sophia quit her dance class to spend time with him—until she began bringing work home with her and reading novels. After several months Dan decided he was not going to allow Sophia's aloofness to keep him from having a good time. At first he stayed longer at work, but that hardly felt like fun. He began going out with his single work friends who liked to play pool and darts at the local pub. At least now Dan was getting to laugh a little. How could he know that Jessica, the sister of a friend, would take such a liking to him? He found their long talks which had evolved into long, intimate walks—exciting and engaging. Dan decided he needed to tell Sophia what was happening, even if it meant an uncertain future. But Dan knew he couldn't settle for a marriage without intimacy and fun. Dan said, "If Sophia had been more attentive, we probably wouldn't have ended up in this mess."

"So," observed Ted, "both Dan and Sophia felt like Victims, while at the same time each looked like a Persecutor to the other. The dance of Victim and Persecutor might seem to describe the whole drama dynamic, but it's never a duo. It's a trio, a triangle of disempowerment."

CHAPTER 3

A Drawing
in the Sand

As Ted walked around to the third point of the triangle, I was lost in my own reflections. How often I had fallen into the role of Persecutor. There were times I had insisted someone else was in the wrong; I just knew I *had* to be right. I had often blamed others for the way I felt or for the way things turned out. I didn't like seeing myself as a shadowy Persecutor. It felt better thinking of myself as the innocent Victim.

Ted reached out with the shell toward the upper left corner of the triangle and wrote an *R*.

The Rescuer

"This third role—the one who steps into the dance between Persecutor and Victim—is **Rescuer**. The dictionary defines the verb *rescue* this way: to free from confinement, danger, or evil; to save or deliver. The Rescuer may also try to alleviate or lessen the Victim's fear and other negative feelings.

"Here, too, a Rescuer isn't always a person. Addictions to alcohol or drugs, sexual addiction, workaholism—all the ways we numb out—can rescue the Victim from feeling his or her feelings."

"I know how badly I want to escape from those feelings when I'm in despair," I admitted. "Having one too many bottles of beer, playing just one more computer game, or zoning out with the sports channel might be Rescuers I've used to feel better.

"But it sounds like you're making the Rescuer out to be a bad guy," I added. "Isn't the Rescuer supposed to be a hero, or at least a helper to the Victim?"

"It might seem that way on the surface," Ted responded. "A person who steps into the role of Rescuer usually does so with a sincere intention to help. But think about it: what the Rescuer is doing—often unconsciously—reinforces the Victim's Poor Me perspective, by saying or thinking, 'Poor You.' Same message, different point of view."

Ted pointed to the roles with his walking stick as he spoke. "So you see, instead of helping or supporting the Victim, the Rescuer just increases the Victim's sense of powerlessness. Unwittingly, the Rescuer enables the Victim to stay small, even though this may be the farthest thing from his stated intention. The Victim ends up feeling ashamed and guilty for needing to be rescued and becomes dependent on the Rescuer for a sense of safety.

"Rescuers look like good guys, but their helpful actions often cover up an underlying fear. Rescuers aren't bad, either. But it is fear that motivates them to fly to the rescue.

"Persecutors fear loss of control. Rescuers fear loss of purpose. Rescuers need Victims—someone to protect or fix—to bolster their self-esteem. Rescuing gives them a false sense of superiority that covers their fear of being inadequate. Rescuers get to feel good about themselves, as long as they don't admit that Victims could meet their own needs without them. With Victims to rescue, Rescuers feel justified; they avoid abandonment by being there for others. They foster dependency by becoming indispensable to a Victim's sense of well-being."

"But Ted, now you're making the Rescuer sound like a Persecutor!" I objected.

"You're on to something there," he said. "It's not unusual for a Victim to switch from seeing the Rescuer as a kind of savior to seeing her as a Persecutor who reminds the Victim of his dependency. In reality, the Rescuer avoids becoming a Victim herself—which is the same motive that drives the Persecutor's behavior. The Rescuer, though, is avoiding abandonment and loss of purpose. The Rescuer often sets herself up for disappointment and rejection when a Victim won't do as she advises or doesn't appreciate her help. Then the Rescuer feels like a martyr: one more name for a Victim."

Ted stood up straight and again motioned with his walking stick toward the Drama Triangle he had drawn in the sand.

Ted explained, "The Drama Triangle, made up of these three roles, shows up in many different cultures. It is maintained through stories, movies, and folktales. Many of the classic fairy tales perfectly depict the Drama Triangle. Consider the ancient example of the damsel in distress (Victim) who anxiously awaits her rescue from the villain (Persecutor) by the handsome prince (Rescuer), who is then supposed to protect her throughout a lifetime lived happily ever after.

"It may seem that the tale reaches a happy ending, but in reality the Drama Triangle's pattern ultimately repeats itself. Eventually the prince/husband becomes domineering, and the damsel/wife becomes dependent or grows cold to her savior's advances. The rest of the story—what happens after the illusion of a cheery ever after fades away—is where the Drama Triangle shows its true colors. This dreaded dynamic is all too common in human relationships."

SHIFTING ROLES

"The Drama Triangle is a tangled web," Ted continued. "A person may play any one of these roles, or he may vacillate between them. The roles may be obvious and explicit, or subtle and seductive. The Persecutor can be a crying baby or a two-year-old throwing a tantrum at the grocery store. The Rescuer could be an extra glass of wine, or a friend saying, 'That's awful,' as you complain about what's been done to you.

"The three roles are intertwined. So when a person changes positions, the other people involved must shift their roles, as well."

I saw how my former wife and I had taken turns as Victim and Persecutor. I thought of well-meaning friends who supported each of us as we complained about the other's faults. I thought of a dear friend of mine, too, and I shared his story with Ted.

My friend had married a beautiful woman with two children. When they met, she had been struggling to make ends meet, and the children's father was mostly absent from their lives. My friend was excited about his instant family and enthusiastically embraced his new role of primary provider and stepdad. He had unwittingly become a Rescuer.

As my friend worked to save his damsel from her distress, several years passed, and the children entered that often rocky road of adolescence. He and his wife argued about what it was reasonable to expect from their teenagers. My friend's wife felt he was critical and judgmental of her parenting. But from his perspective, my friend was only offering helpful alternatives. He had maintained his role as Rescuer. What he didn't realize was that his wife had stopped thinking of him as her Rescuer and had now cast him in the role of Persecutor.

My friend's wife sought comfort with friends and coworkers who supported her Victim stance (new Rescuers). She lashed out at him in reaction to her feelings of victimization. When this happened, *he* felt like a Victim to her Persecutor counterattack. The two saw a series of couples' counselors looking for rescue, but their marriage finally ended in divorce.

I added, "He was depressed and withdrawn for months after that."

"It's true," said Ted, "these dramas often lead to despair. There may be times of relative stability, of course, when it seems things are under control. But living in this drama means staying alert for anything or anyone that might threaten that fragile stability. Everyone is on the defensive. Victim defends herself against Persecutor. Rescuer defends Victim from Persecutor. Persecutor defends himself against Rescuer. Exhausting!

"When you inhabit any of these three roles, you're reacting to fear of Victimhood, loss of control, or loss of purpose. You're always looking outside yourself, to the people and circumstances of life, for a sense of safety, security, and sanity.

"When you consider your past, which seems to be filled with Victims, Persecutors, and Rescuers, you assume that the future will be much the same. Since you've been a Victim before, you project that into the future, working to prevent or put off what you believe is your inevitable Victimhood. Living this way is like driving while looking only in the rearview mirror. You assume the road ahead will be just like the road behind you.

"When you accept this as the way things are, the chance of the Dreaded Drama Triangle repeating itself dramatically increases. These beliefs are often formed quite early in life. They've been with you so long, you're completely unaware of them—and their power."

I looked out at the ocean and took in Ted's words. They felt like a tidal wave that engulfed me, as I saw how much of my life reflected the turmoil of the Drama Dynamic.

Ted continued, "Ultimately, the Drama Dynamic results in spiritual destruction. As you resign yourself to the inevitability of the pattern, your spirit suffers and gradually withers. Perhaps that's why so many people suffer from depression. One absorbed in the Drama Dynamic sleepwalks through her days, believing that this nightmare is just the way things are.

"It's a toxic mutation of the human relationship, and it pains me to see it played out so often. I call it the Dreaded Drama Triangle—the DDT. Do you know about DDT?"

"Isn't that the poisonous chemical they used for years to kill insects, the one that was later banned in most parts of the world?" I said.

"Yes. It is a toxin. Banning the poisonous Dreaded Drama Triangle—the DDT—from the affairs of human-kind would make the world a saner and safer place, too, don't you think?"

Just then I heard the crashing of a wave on the beach. Glancing out at the ocean, I realized that the tide had turned. Ted noticed, too.

He said, "Before the tide comes back in, there's one more thing I want you to know about. Let's move up there to those rocks. I'll show you the atmosphere the DDT thrives in. It's called the Victim Orientation."

CHAPTER 4

THE VICTIM ORIENTATION

As Ted and I continued up the beach, I scanned the bluff above us. Only a few minutes ago I had been sitting on that bench, eyes closed in surrender and prayer, when this stranger showed up beside me. Now here we were deep in conversation about the very concerns that had made me drop everything and take a vacation to mull over this turning point in my life. I barely had an inkling of the giant turnaround I was about to make.

We walked away from the water to several large rocks that jutted out of the beach near the bluff. Ted's picture of the Dreaded Drama Triangle was still etched in my mind.

"Let's sit down on this big rock here," Ted suggested.

We sat next to one another, much like we had been

sitting on the bench. Ted leaned his staff against the
back of the stone. As we sat in silence for a few minutes,
I could still see his drawing in the sand out near the
water.

"The DDT is one way to get a bird's-eye view of your
life. The dramas we've been talking about are just one
part of it: the end result of your personal Orientation to
the world," said Ted.

"Orientation? What do you mean, exactly?" I asked.

"An Orientation is a point of reference, a mental
standpoint that determines your direction. Have you
ever worked with a compass?"

"Sure, I used one when I was a Boy Scout. But that's
been a while!" I laughed.

"Well," said
Ted, "you know
how a compass
gives you a point
of reference by
indicating which way
is north? Using that knowledge you can set a course,
decide which way you want to go. An
Orientation works like a compass—one that's inside

you. Your inner Orientation, your mental standpoint, has a lot to do with the direction you take in life. So your Orientation determines a lot of what you experience. The dictionary says that an orientation is a general or lasting direction of thought, inclination, or interest."

"Okay. Orientation. Point of reference. Direction. I think I get it, but what does that have to do with being a Victim?" I asked.

"What you focus on (your Orientation) determines how you act. It affects just about everything that shows up in your life, too. So the DDT is the direct result of having a Victim Orientation to the world. I'll show you what I mean."

FINDING THE FISBE

Ted turned to face me. "I assume that is a journal in your hand."

"Yes," I said. "I was writing in it right before you joined me up there on the bench."

"It's a nice one. If it's all right with you, I'd like to draw a couple of illustrations that I think you will find useful."

I pulled the pen from the clasp, opened the journal to the next blank page, and handed it to Ted. He accepted it from me and drew three circles on the page. The circles were arranged in a sort of triangle: one at the top and two at the bottom. Then he said something really weird. "I call this one a *Fizz-bee.*"

I knew I couldn't have heard him correctly. "You mean a *Frisbee*?" I asked.

Ted laughed and pointed up the beach to where a young man and woman were tossing a plastic disk back and forth. "No, not a toy. A *FISBE. FISBE* stands for these three circles here." Ted wrote the letter *F* in the top circle. "*F* stands for the Focus of your Orientation. Now, whatever you focus on is going to cause you to have some sort of emotional response. Just look at the ocean for a minute, David. When you focus on the waves out there, what kind of feelings do you have?"

The waves were rising, cresting, dissolving into the shore, leaving dark demarcations where they sank into the sand. I breathed deeply, taking in the whole scene. "Serenity," I said, almost without thinking. "There's all that power and this huge expanse of blue. That's why I come out here. Being near the ocean gives me a sense of calm. I need that calm feeling to get some perspective."

"Great. Your Focus on the ocean evokes a particular Inner State." Ted drew an arrow down diagonally from the top circle and connected it to the circle on the right. In that circle, he wrote *IS*. "Your Inner State right now is calm and serene."

Ted continued, "Your Focus creates your Inner State—and that Inner State motivates you to act a certain way. Right now your Focus is on the ocean, and it evokes in you an Inner State of serenity. When you feel that kind of calm, what do you do? How do you act when you're here at the beach?"

I looked back up the bluff to the bench where I had come to sit. "I become contemplative," I said. "When I first get to the beach, I usually stand still or sit down, like I did up there, and just look out to sea. Then everything seems to slow down, and before I know it, I'm thinking more deeply about my whole life. That's how I get perspective."

As I spoke, Ted drew another arrow, this time from the second circle to the one at the bottom left. In that circle, he wrote *Be*. "Great! *Be* stands for Behavior. So your slowing down and getting contemplative is how you Behave when you calmly Focus on the ocean. You've just given a perfect example of FISBE in action!"

I looked at Ted's diagram on the page in my journal. "So, my Focus engages me in an emotional Inner State that drives my **Be**havior—is that it?"

"Exactly!" exclaimed Ted. "Your Orientation sets in motion your experience: how you Behave in life. The Dreaded Drama Triangle is the result of a certain Orientation: the Victim Orientation. Let's look at the FISBE for that one."

Ted then drew another three similar circles below the FISBE. "In the Victim Orientation, the Focus is on a problem in your life." (In the top circle, he wrote *Problem*.)

"Like when a Victim focuses on the Persecutor?" I ventured.

"You got it! Or when a Persecutor looks down on the Victim and sees that person as a problem."

PROBLEM ▸ ANXIETY ▸ REACTION

Ted continued, "Even a Rescuer focuses on the Victim as a problem person who needs help. Remember, the problem can be a person, a condition, or a circumstance in your life."

I recalled how I had focused on my infertility, my divorce, and my dad's death as problems.

In the second circle Ted wrote *Anxiety*. "When a problem shows up, you feel anxiety: the Inner State of the Victim Orientation. The intensity of the anxiety might be anything from mild discomfort or annoyance to sheer terror. Anxiety—whether mild or intense—gives you energy for action and sparks your behavior. How you behave is always a kind of reaction."

He wrote *Reaction* in the third circle. "Sound familiar?"

"Now I'll bet you're going to say that the reaction is either *fight, flee, or freeze!*" I said.

"Hey, you're a fast learner!" Ted smiled warmly.

"That's all too familiar, I have to admit," I said, pointing at the diagram in my journal.

"I'm sure it is," he said. "Indeed, the Victim

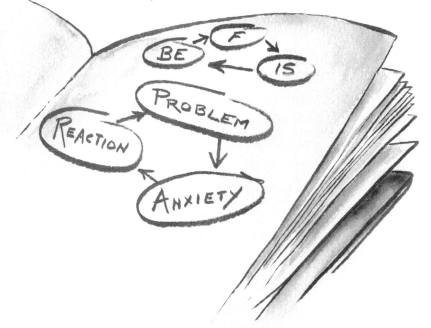

Orientation is the approach that most human beings take toward their experience, by default. You spend a lot of time searching for solutions to problems. Problems are often the center of people's lives."

"That sure has been my experience lately," I said. "When I used to go back and forth between walking on eggshells and blaming my wife, I saw both her and our relationship as problems. There was so much fear and anger and hurt—a lot of anxiety, I guess, like you said. My reactions went from doing whatever I could to keep things smoothed over to outright anger and blame.

"I can see the Dreaded Drama Triangle in my own life," I continued. "Each of the three roles sees the other ones as *problems* that need to be solved. There's plenty of anxiety, and it goes around and around between them, which leads to their reactions. And that creates the drama. Looks like this cycle could go on forever!"

"Yes, it certainly does," Ted said. "The DDT cycle is very difficult to break—but not impossible. To find the way out, you start by recognizing two important things about the Victim Orientation: The first one is a delusion that lies at the center of this Orientation. The second is a false hope that can never be fulfilled as long as the cycle continues."

DELUSION AND FALSE HOPE

I could see that Ted was on a roll, and I was riveted. I knew that if I wanted to get out of the Victim Orientation, I was going to have to get a grip on this delusion he was talking about, and the false hope that went with it.

Ted went on. "Let's look first at the delusion. Let me ask you a question. When you react to something, what do you tell yourself you are reacting to—the problem or the anxiety?"

I hesitated. "Well," I said, "I think I'm reacting to the problem. I mean, if the problem didn't exist, I wouldn't be reacting that way."

Ted pointed toward the diagram of the Victim Orientation. "Okay, now look at the FISBE. Consider those three pieces—Focus, Inner State, and Behavior. Which one gets your reaction going?"

"According to the FISBE, it looks like I'm reacting to the anxiety: my Inner State," I said.

"Right! The anxiety you feel comes from your way of focusing on the problem. That's your Inner State, and that is what actually drives your Behavior. You may be feeling anxious because the problem exists, but

45

the anxiety itself is not the problem. You're anxious because of the state you're in. So here's the delusion of the Victim Orientation: you believe you're reacting to a problem, when you are really reacting to your own anxiety."

"So what's your point, Ted? I'm not sure I follow . . ."

"Good question. For one thing, it's important to know that it is your anxiety—based in fear—that moves you to act when you're in the Victim Orientation. If you don't feel anxious, you lose your motivation to do anything about it. So with a Victim Orientation, in a strange way you actually need a problem to get moving! To see why this is so important, look at how each part of the FISBE creates a pattern of behavior with its own results.

"Let's start with the Focus: a problem. When your wife became distant, what happened to your anxiety? Did it increase or decrease?"

"When she did that, I felt more anxious . . . definitely," I said.

"Right. And when your anxiety increases, what happens to your tendency to react?"

"Well," I said, "my desire to react also increases—I want to get rid of the anxiety."

"Okay, David. This next step is critical. If your reaction is successful—meaning that it has a positive impact on your problem—what happens to the intensity of the problem?"

"The problem seems less intense, if I do something that seems to help."

"Good," said Ted. "Now watch this: When the problem seems less intense, what happens to your anxiety?"

"It goes down. Things don't seem so bad."

"When the anxiety lessens, what happens to your feeling that you've got to do something about the problem?"

"It goes down, too," I said. "I relax and take a deep breath."

"Of course you would. Now here's where the delusion comes into play. Remember when I said that in the Victim Orientation, it's actually your anxiety that motivates you to take action? Well, when your anxiety goes away, so does your energy for taking action. So what happens if your drive to take action against the problem lessens? What will eventually happen to the intensity of that problem?"

"Well," I said, "the problem might still be lurking around, kind of like a disease that's gone into remission.

I'm guessing the problem would most likely reemerge, and so, eventually, it would seem *more* intense. Right?"

"Right!" Ted exclaimed. "And when that intensity about the problem reemerges, the whole cycle restarts itself. It's déjà vu all over again, as somebody once said. Any problem that seems to come up in your life again and again—whether it's with an employee, coworker, a loved one, or even within yourself—is virtually guaranteed to get you involved in the Victim Orientation. You do something about the situation, it gets better for awhile, and it then recurs sometime down the road. It may take days, weeks, months, maybe even years, but it's a safe bet that the problem will raise its head again in the future."

"Wait! I'm not sure I get it. Why does the intensity of the problem go up again? Didn't I solve the problem when I reacted to it the first time?" I asked.

"Almost never," Ted explained. "A problem is rarely if ever solved from within Victim Orientation. To truly eliminate the source of a problem usually takes a long-term focus. In the Victim Orientation that kind of focus is almost impossible, because when things do get better, you lose that get-up-and-go energy to do something about the problem. Things get better and you relax and stop reacting to the problem, only to find it starting up all over again."

"Yikes."

"No kidding! This recurring pattern can last for years and years, highs and then lows, more highs and then more lows. I've heard plenty of people say their lives are like a roller coaster. So, David, what do you think? Have you ever fallen into this pattern?"

I gazed out at the approaching waves, trying to think of a time when I'd been on the kind of roller coaster drama that Ted was describing. I felt a little flustered, but I was determined. There had to be a way out of this Victim cycle. I took a deep breath, looked down at my stomach, and let out a long sigh. Then it struck me.

"Sure," I chuckled. "It may sound a little silly, but it seems like I've always been on a roller coaster with my weight. The **problem** shows up when I step on the scale in the morning. When I look down at the scale, there's just a mild **anxiety**, but I feel the weight of that number staring back at me between my feet. I **react** by promising myself to diet and exercise. I stay focused and committed for awhile. I start to lose pounds and inches, and pretty soon I'm feeling really great. My clothes fit better. My friends and family tell me how good I'm looking. But then something comes up, like a big holiday or a vacation. And because things are going so well, I celebrate by eating all the things I've been avoiding. The problem is that afterward I don't go back to my healthy eating or exercising. After awhile, one day I'm standing on the same scale on a whole new morning wondering how all those problem pounds came back."

Ted smiled sympathetically. "You got it! That's how the Victim Orientation works. Your example may be ordinary, but unfortunately it's exactly the same cycle that shows up in much more serious situations like addiction, when someone quits and then has a relapse. In situations of domestic violence and abusive relationships, a Persecutor or perpetrator hurts a Victim, then apologizes and pledges to not do it again. Things may seem to go well for awhile, only to end in some explosive incident that starts the cycle all over again."

DDT and Victim Orientation: A Perfect Match

"You see," Ted continued, "the Dreaded Drama Triangle is rooted in the Victim Orientation: look at the roles and their reactions. Imagine you're the Victim in the triangle. Remember, in the DDT there are only three possible reactions: fight, flee, or freeze. The Victim may lash out to fight back when faced with a Persecutor. When that happens, the Victim becomes the Persecutor and the original Persecutor now becomes the Victim. Or the Victim may flee to get away from the Persecutor, striking out in search of a Rescuer who will welcome the Victim with open arms.

"Or the Victim may freeze. The freeze reaction can be to do nothing, but that usually isn't what happens. More often, the Victim finds a way to numb out the fear and pain of Victimhood. Numbing out can be done in any number of ways—most of them addictive—like drugs or alcohol, working too much, zoning out in front of the television, or anything else that offers escape from feelings. All three reactions—fight, flee, or freeze—are reactions to the problem presented by the Persecutor."

I could see how consistently the DDT and the reactive cycle of the Victim Orientation had played out in my own life. "This has happened to me so many times," I said. "Like, all my life I've been afraid other people will leave me. I can think of lots of times when I was a Victim of abandonment, both emotionally and physically, and I lost an important relationship. Whenever this happened, I had a flight reaction: right away I started looking for another relationship to fill the emptiness."

"That new relationship became your Rescuer—saving you from the pain you felt when you were left alone," Ted responded.

"Right. This fear of abandonment has given me a kind of supersensitive radar. I'm constantly looking for signs that the other person is going to leave or that the good things in my life will be taken away. I start reacting to every possible clue that something is about to go wrong. I hate to say it, but I get clingy. I hold on so tightly and focus so intently on the relationship that other people start feeling smothered or pressured. They then react by getting distant from me."

"And as that person grows distant, you see her as your Persecutor," said Ted. "Right?"

"You bet!" I exclaimed. "She becomes my newest abandoner—my Persecutor—and the cycle starts all over again, just like you said. That's what happened between my wife and me. When I found out about my infertility, I wanted more and more reassurance from her, but that only drove her further away. I sure wish I had known about all this back then."

"Your story illustrates another important part of the Victim Orientation, David. Much of humanity is sleepwalking through life—moving through the day firmly rooted in the Victim Orientation and not being aware of it. It accounts for much of the tragedy of the human experience."

Ted turned away a moment and looked out at the approaching waves. He picked up a gnarled stick of driftwood and threw it onto the sand near the waterline. Just then a huge wave arose, submerged the stick, and carried it away. As we watched it bob away on the water's surface, I glanced at Ted. A faraway look was in his eyes. He took a breath and continued. "When sleepwalking, you constantly react to problems, even to your own behaviors. In the Victim Orientation, you want to get rid of, or get away from, your problems. But often the things you do to try to make the problem (or the Persecutor) go away just end up intensifying your suffering."

"Actually, there were times when things seemed to be going okay," said. "I mean, sometimes my wife and I got along all right, and we had a kind of peaceful coexistence, even if we weren't all that happy."

"The Victim Orientation can be very seductive," said Ted. "As long as your reaction—be it fight, flee, or freeze—seems to make the situation better (like that period of peaceful coexistence), you tell yourself that your reaction is working to get you what you want. In your case that meant feeling safe and avoiding loneliness. But then, just as you described, at some point you noticed your wife getting distant, and you reacted by pushing for more closeness. Instead of solving the problem your reaction made it worse, as she began to feel smothered and pressured.

"So, reacting actually increases the problem. When that happens, life quickly becomes a slippery slope. The problem worsens, and your anxiety increases. As the anxiety increases, you act out to reduce your anxiety. That acting out—clinging or begging or shouting in frustration—only throws fuel onto the fire."

"I get it," I sighed. "My own fearful reaction creates the exact result I'm trying so hard to avoid: being abandoned."

"Exactly," Ted confirmed. "Then you go on to the next relationship and play out the same drama, unless or until you wake up to what you're doing. As long as you're sleepwalking, you're unaware of this cycle. While you're playing out the drama, you don't see that what you're doing is counterproductive—because, at first, your reactions seem to be working to keep your anxiety down."

Ted looked squarely at me. "While sleepwalking, you think your problem is out there to be fixed, not realizing how your own reactions contribute to your suffering. You believe the pain exists out there in your environment, and that if you can just fix that—through fighting, fleeing, or freezing—life will get better."

"Okay," I said. "I get how I keep the cycle going and how my Victim stance feeds the drama. But what about someone else, someone who really is a Victim of circumstances beyond his control?"

"Oh yes. War and murder, starvation . . . While it's true that certain circumstances are not of your own making, it is also true that the way you react to those circumstances—usually by trying to make it all go away—becomes the source of even more suffering and keeps the cycle active."

The ocean waves were now growing in size. We watched the tide rolling in, and a wave began to build and grow. The wave crested, breaking toward the shore; it crashed into the sand . . . and wiped away the Dreaded Drama Triangle Ted had drawn. He turned to me. "What an apt metaphor. The wave just wiped out the DDT! I wish it was that easy to overcome the limitations of that way of being in the world. But the

Victim Orientation is ancient. It has been humanity's primary orientation for as long as we have roamed the earth. The urge to fight, flee, or freeze has played an important survival role, a vital evolutionary force. The tough reality is that the Victim Orientation and its mischievous dynamics will always be a part of you. But the Victim Orientation has outgrown its usefulness, David. It doesn't have to drive your life and relationships anymore."

I searched Ted's eyes for clues. How could he be so certain? "So, are you saying that I don't have to react to trouble?" It seemed unlikely.

"That's right," he said. "There is another Orientation that presents a different choice, one that can only be made consciously. That next evolutionary leap will take you to a very different Orientation. But we'll talk about that later."

The waves were growing in intensity. Little by little, the beach seemed to be shrinking. My mind was reeling from all that Ted had told me. He smiled. "Perhaps the rest can wait. Can you come back tomorrow?"

"Yes," I answered. "I'm taking some time off right now. I had planned on spending a few days out here, anyway. I'd like to hear more. When could we get together?"

"How about meeting at the bench up there on the bluff around mid-morning? Whenever you want to show up is fine by me."

"I'll see you in the morning, then." I said.

CHAPTER 5

ANOTHER FRIEND

I sat on the bench at mid-morning, staring out at the ocean. The sun had burned off the coastal layer of fog, and the water, stretching out like a blanket buffeted by the wind, covered the earth.

My sleep had been restless. All night Ted's teachings had churned through my brain like the waves crashing onto the beach below. It was a huge burden, realizing how much of my life had been spent caught up in the Victim Orientation. How many times had I traveled around the DDT, that toxic Dreaded Drama Triangle? As I lay awake in bed, my mind wandered from the mundane to the monumental, considering all the highs and lows of my life in light of this new viewpoint.

A few days earlier my flight to the coast had been delayed in Chicago, and like the other passengers, I was anxious to get where I was going. We were all victims of the weather that day, and the havoc it had wreaked on the flow of airport arrivals and departures. I remember how some travelers approached the gate agents as potential Rescuers, as if the buttons on their computer keypads could accomplish instant magic. When the ticket agents promised that they would only announce new information when it became available, I watched those same passengers begin treating the agents as Persecutors.

When had I first taken up the Victim Orientation? I guess it went back to my early family life. No doubt my parents had loved me and did the best they could, but they had unwittingly repeated certain unhealthy patterns from their own upbringing. I suppose if I followed the genealogical map of the Victim Orientation, it would lead all the way back to early humans and the fight, flee, or freeze reactions that had helped them survive to populate the world. And now evolution had placed me at this critical choice point: I had the opportunity to break the Victim cycle, to stop the patterns that passed it on from generation to generation. The prospect was overwhelming.

I was also excited. Something new was about to happen! There was a more fulfilling way of being in the world after all, and I knew that today Ted would give me some clues about how to live it. Or so I hoped. We had left things fairly open-ended the day before. What if he didn't show up? I had no phone number, no way to contact Ted. I took a deep breath of salt air and let it go. I decided to trust the process.

I closed my eyes and offered a prayer of gratitude. I had found a wise friend, and now I had the time to consider our conversation, maybe even start putting it all to good use. I took a slow, full breath. The salt air and the sound of waves on the shore blended with the calls of seagulls overhead. The breeze brushed my cheek. I felt calm, at peace.

Ted cleared his throat. I opened my eyes and there he was, standing with his staff in hand. I had not even heard him approach. He smiled. I nodded. We were ready to begin again.

MOVING BEYOND THE VICTIM STORY

I tucked my journal under my arm and we started toward the path. Silently we made our way down to the beach, and this time I managed not to fall. As we passed the point where I had slipped the day before, Ted noticed the difference.

"I see you stayed upright—congratulations!" Ted observed. "You walked differently just now as you approached the place where you slipped yesterday."

"I guess I learned from the experience," I chuckled. "I was a lot more aware of that spot today, so I came at it a little differently."

"You learned from your experience. You stayed aware of the lessons of yesterday's fall, and that gave you the option to choose a new approach just now. That's what I want to explore with you today. There is a different approach to your life that will serve you much better than the DDT and the Victim Orientation," said Ted. Then he went on, "What a fine day!"

And it was: clear sky, a brilliant sun, and the tide moving out to reveal the smooth sand that had served as Ted's blackboard the day before. My pace quickened as we reached the edge of the shore. As the waves lapped and smoothed over the sand, I noticed a woman in the distance who seemed to be looking our way. She waved and started walking toward us.

Ted turned to me and said, "I've invited someone to join us, David. Her name is Sophia. A couple of years ago we met on this beach and had much the same conversation that you and I had yesterday."

Sophia smiled and gave Ted a hug. She kissed him on the cheek, and he held her at arm's length, studying her face. "It's been a while, my friend," he said.

Sophia's hazel eyes sparkled. "It's been too long. Not a day goes by, though, that I don't think of you." I studied Sophia. Her light auburn hair fell around her shoulders, blowing in the sea breeze. She reached into her beach bag and brought out a baseball cap and an exercise band. In one swift motion, she pulled on the cap to tame her hair and placed the stretchy band around her wrist. Then she turned to me.

"And you must be David," she said warmly. Before I knew it, she had taken both my hands in hers. With a penetrating look, she said, "You're a fortunate one to have met Ted, you know. That bench up there is a magical spot."

"You met Ted there too, then? I think he told me a little about your story yesterday. When did you two meet?" I asked.

"A little over two years ago. I had just split up with my husband, Dan."

I nodded. "There seems to be a pattern here: marriages and relationships coming to an end."

"It's no accident that Ted brought us together today. He tends to do that," Sofia replied, smiling. "So often people come to a point in their lives where they are ready to make a significant change and it is helpful to benefit from the experience of others who have been down a similar path. For some, like you and me, it is through close relationships that perhaps are no longer working. But Ted has met other people who found their way out of Victimhood for different reasons and in different aspects of their lives. Some were fed up with office politics or had hit bottom in their addictions. Others had breakdowns in their families or while facing death. The ways people arrive at this choice point are as varied as the human experience."

A young couple walked by arm in arm, oblivious to us on their romantic walk down the beach. I felt an inner tug of envy and a stab of loneliness. "Tell me more about yourself, Sophia."

"I assume that Ted mentioned my husband, Dan, and how he had an affair," Sophia answered. "I could say that was the reason we divorced, but that would only be a half-truth, because I was doing the other half of the DDT dance. There was so much hurt and anger in our relationship those last few months. We had created

a pretty abusive, toxic environment—a vicious cycle of playing out those same dynamics again and again.

"But I don't talk about that much anymore," she continued. "It's not who I am now, so I rarely tell those old Victimhood stories." Sophia glanced at Ted.

"Sophia is referring to something of vital importance, David. The way you talk about yourself and your life—your story—has a great deal to do with what shows up in your day-to-day experience. Your thoughts create filters through which you view your life. If you think of yourself as a Victim, you filter all that happens to you through the lens of the DDT, and you find plenty of evidence to support that viewpoint. That's why the orientation you adopt is so important: it exerts a powerful influence on your life direction."

"I'm very clear about not wanting to live my life from the Victim Orientation anymore," I said. "But you've got to tell me: what's the alternative? I stayed awake for hours last night contemplating everything we talked about. There's got to be an alternative to the DDT and the Victim Orientation."

Now Ted and Sophia were both smiling at me.

"Well?" I said, a little impatient.

"The opposite of Victim is Creator," said Ted.

I did a double take. Ted's answer echoed the response I had heard from within myself just the day before. Had I imagined it? Just what was going on here?

CHAPTER 6

THE CREATOR ORIENTATION

Did Ted know that I already knew? *The opposite of Victim is Creator.* That insight had reverberated within me just yesterday as I sat on the bench praying for answers. Those words had burned themselves into my mind only moments before I discovered Ted sitting beside me. Probably just a coincidence.

"The change Ted is pointing to, moving from Victim to Creator, is a fundamental shift of mind," Sophia said. "To explain, let me share just a bit more about what happened in my marriage to Dan. As our relationship headed into a downward spiral, I began to feel as if nothing I did was ever enough. I had quit my dance class, which I really loved, to spend more time with him. But then he objected when I brought work home or relaxed with a book. He wanted more attention than I could give, I guess. It turned out that the way I naturally behaved in our relationship just wasn't what he wanted or needed. I was despondent about the whole situation. The day I came to sit on that bench, I was trying to get a handle on my life and my future direction."

Sophia paused and looked out at the rolling waves, reliving the moment.

"Once I met up with Ted and we began talking about the DDT," she continued, "I saw how deeply I believed I wasn't enough. Cycling through the DDT and Victim Orientation over and over again reinforced this belief for me. Now, this is where the Creator part comes in: Ted helped me to see that whatever I hold in my mind tends to manifest itself in my life. What we believe and assume creates most of our reality and our experience, David. I'll bet you and Ted talked about some of your core beliefs yesterday."

"Yes," I said. "Yesterday I came face-to-face with an old belief of mine: that I'm a problem and that people will always abandon me. I'm pretty sure I know when it all started . . ."

Smiling, Sophia listened for a few minutes as I described the situations that I believed had led to my clingy fear of abandonment, my pattern of lashing out, even my persistent weight challenge. After a little while Sophia put one hand up, signaling she'd heard enough.

"I don't mean to be rude, David, but you know what? It's not so important to me to hear the stories of your past. I'm much more interested in thinking about the new stories you're going to create when you begin using what Ted's going to show you today. Once you have this knowledge, life will never look the same to you again. Tomorrow will be like a fresh canvas on which you'll paint your unique contribution to your world."

I turned toward Ted. He reached out toward my journal, which I held in my hand. "May I?" he asked. "There's another Orientation I'd like to draw. Let's walk back up to the rocks we were on yesterday."

"Are you going to toss me another FISBE?" I grinned.

Ted laughed. "Yes, but it's miles apart from yesterday's FISBE. It has a different Focus, a much different Inner State, and leads to a whole new set of Behaviors."

The three of us settled comfortably on the rocks near the bluff. Ted opened the journal and turned to the page next to the one on which he had drawn the FISBE and Victim Orientation the day before. He drew yet another set of three circles.

"The focus in the Creator Orientation is on a Vision or an Outcome. You orient your thoughts and actions toward creating what you most want to see or experience in life. Sometimes the vision or outcome may be completely clear to you. At other times it may be vague, only a general idea about where you want to go."

As he spoke, Ted wrote *Vision* and *Outcome* in the top circle of the FISBE.

"For the first few months after I met Ted," Sophia interjected, "my vision was solely to live each day from the standpoint of the Creator Orientation. In a practical sense, I didn't really know what this was going to mean. I just knew that it was the direction I wanted for my life. Placing my attention on outcomes rather than on problems has made a world of difference. That one choice has had a powerful impact on every single area of my life."

Ted added, "One of the fundamental differences between the Victim Orientation and this one is where you put the focus of your attention, as Sophia mentioned. For Victims, the focus is always on what they don't want: the problems that seem constantly to multiply in their lives. They don't want the person, condition, or circumstance they consider to be their Persecutor, and they don't want the fear that leads to fight, flee, or freeze reactions, either. Creators, on the other hand, place their focus on what they do want. Doing this, Creators still face and solve problems in the course of creating the outcomes they want, but their focus remains fixed on their ultimate vision."

I recalled a quote from the Bible that someone had recently shared with me. Something like, "Where there is no vision, the people perish." As I stood with Ted and Sophia, I felt the importance of this concept. I was quite clear that I didn't want to live from the Victim stance anymore, but I was not yet clear about what I wanted to create. Growing up, I had learned all too well how to focus on problems. It seemed that was always the focus in my family: not enough money, not enough time, my parents arguing, relatives who were sick or struggling. . . . After a few moments of silence, I looked over at Sophia and Ted.

"I find that I know all too well what I *don't* want in my life. I'm not sure how to get clear about what I *do* want," I said.

"That is quite often the case when we've been sleepwalking through life in the Victim Orientation," Sophia responded. "When we lack vision for what we want in our lives, seeing only what we don't want, the unique contribution that we're here to offer seems to vanish. In that dark place we often can't see our way out. We hardly know which way is forward. Those first few months that Ted and I talked, all I could focus on was the Creator Orientation itself. I also spent quite a bit of time exploring what I most wanted to contribute to others. Later we can talk more about discerning our life's meaning and purpose. But first I want Ted to finish outlining the Creator Orientation. Ted?"

"Thanks, Sophia. I really like hearing your story, especially what's happened for you in the last couple of years. It makes my heart sing! David, this 'singing of the heart' is the quality of the Inner State of the Creator Orientation. As you focus on your envisioned outcomes, you connect with forgotten or seldom-felt emotions: passion, love, a sense of your heart's desire."

Ted wrote *Passion* in the center of the second circle in the journal. He said, "When you focus on those things in your life that hold meaning and purpose, your passion just naturally flows."

"Can you remember a time in your life when passion, desire, or love just naturally arose?" Sophia asked.

I thought for a moment. "Well sure," I said. "Before

my wife and I were married, when we were dating. We spent a lot of time just hanging out together. Back then I only had to look at her, and those feelings just began washing over me."

"Hmm," said Ted. "You may not want to hear this David, but that feeling may actually be more related to your experience in the Victim Orientation than to what we're after here. I would bet the feelings you identified then as love were also the result of your having found your next Rescuer. Do you see how that might be possible?"

I frowned. I felt a tug at the pit of my stomach. "Yeah, I guess so. But being in a relationship is what I really wanted."

Sophia added, "David, Ted's making an important point. Of course you wanted a relationship. People naturally seek out intimate relationships. But wanting a relationship to chase away your loneliness is very different from consciously envisioning the qualities and characteristics of the kind of person with whom you want to create a partnership. In my own case, as I approached dating from the Creator Orientation—after many, many months of healing after my divorce—I became much more discerning. I spent a lot of time clarifying, with the help of a coach and mentor, the qualities and characteristics of the kind of person I wanted to be in a committed relationship with. When feelings of love and passion began to emerge with my new partner, Jake, I knew those feelings had come up not because Jake was 'the right partner,' but because I was consciously choosing to see in him the qualities I most wanted in a partner.

"So, David," Sophia continued. "Let me ask again: Can you think of a time in which passion or desire arose naturally, aside from the early stages of a relationship? Take a few minutes and look back over your life."

I remembered my first job out of college. "Right after I finished college I got a really exciting job helping to build a public access cable television studio and opera-tion. We built the whole thing with our own hands. I trained volunteers how to use video equipment and edit programs. We had in-studio programs to educate and reach out to the public, we taped area events, and we all felt that we were helping to build real community. We won national awards for our efforts. I would wake up every morning eager to get to work, to begin the day's new creations. It didn't pay much, but it was one of the most fun and exciting jobs I've ever had."

Sophia smiled and said, "If you could only see your eyes right now, David. Your lights are on and burning brightly. That's how passion looks and feels in the Creator Orientation."

"When you tap that passion to create the outcomes that matter to you, it provides powerful energy to take action toward your heart's desires," said Ted. "The behavior that moves you in that direction is taking Baby Steps. Taking a Baby Step means doing the next logical thing in front of you—making a phone call, having a conversation, or gathering information. Each step you take either moves you closer to your vision or helps you clarify the final form of your desired outcome."

Ted wrote *Baby Steps* in the last circle. "It is the Baby Steps you take, the everyday things you do, that eventually lead to the manifestation of your outcome."

"That makes sense," I said. "I did that same thing again and again when I worked in the cable television studio. I used to love the editing process. We'd usually record more than twice the amount of footage we would need for a final videotape. Then I'd sit in the editing room for hours putting the program together one scene at a time, like a video jigsaw puzzle. I never thought of calling it *Baby Steps*, but that is definitely the process we were using to produce TV programs."

THREE BIG DIFFERENCES

"Whether you're creating a television program, building a house, or beginning a new relationship, the basic process is the same," Sophia said. "The Creator Orientation is a powerful and simple—although not always easy—way to think and act. It has become very important to me, thanks to Ted."

"You're welcome, Sophia." Ted smiled. "There is definitely a different AIR about you since you've adopted the Creator Orientation. I can assure you, David, that people who know you will soon begin to notice a different AIR about you, too, if you commit to the Creator Orientation as your primary stance in life."

"Ted's hinting at the three things that make the difference

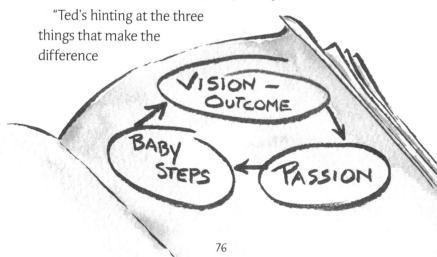

between the Victim and The Creator Orientation," Sophia added, chuckling. "Ted, stop being a goofball and tell David what AIR stands for!"

Ted winked at me. His smile activated little creases in his face, and his eyes glistened. "AIR stands for three big differences between the Victim and Creator stances. The first is where you place your **Attention**. As the Victim, your focus is on what you don't want: you think, speak, and act on the problems in your life. As Creator, you place your attention first and foremost on what you do want: your envisioned outcome.

"The second difference is your **Intention**. In the Victim Orientation your intention is to get rid of, or away from, your problems. In the Creator Orientation your intention is to bring into being, or manifest, the outcomes you envision.

"The third big difference is the **Results** you produce. The results of the Victim Orientation are temporary and reactive. With the Creator Orientation, though, you're much more likely to produce satisfying, sustainable results over time. With each Baby Step you take from the Creator stance, you come closer to—or get clearer about—your heart's desires."

Sophia chimed in, "Don't think that Ted's saying the

Creator Orientation is all sweetness and light, or that there's no such thing as a problem. I can tell you from experience that living from the Creator Orientation is actually more challenging. In the Victim Orientation, I didn't have to exercise conscious choice: I just reacted to my circumstances. The Creator Orientation requires considering and choosing my response to everything that happens; taking many, many Baby Steps that eventually lead to manifesting my envisioned outcome. And in the process, problems certainly do come up."

Ted continued, "In the Creator Orientation, however, you cultivate the capacity to choose which problems get your attention. You select problems that will best serve your outcomes—and those are the only problems you actively work to solve.

"It's important to know that even when you adopt the Creator Orientation you'll still experience anxiety at times. As Sophia said so well, the Creator Orientation is not all sweetness and light. Anxiety and fear are a natural and normal part of our experience. Creators, however, learn how to move forward in their lives with courage in the face of fear and anxiety. And there are no guarantees. Often you won't know whether your heart's desires are attainable until after you've put in a great deal of time, effort, and experimentation to make your envisioned outcome a reality."

Sophia added, "After Dan and I had been apart for awhile, I eventually chose to be open to another intimate relationship. As I began dating, exploring what I wanted in a relationship, I came up against a lot of fear and anxiety. Sometimes I thought the conscious, co-creative bond I was hoping for was just a romantic fantasy. I dated a number of men before I met Jake. Each person I met, and each experience I had while I was dating, helped me get clearer about the kind of relationship I wanted."

A flock of pelicans flew along the shoreline just a few feet above the surf. As I followed their flight, I wondered how long it would be before I was willing and ready to be open to a new relationship. I shuddered at the thought. I also felt a twinge of sadness as I realized I was much more certain about what I didn't want in my life than I was about what I wanted to create. Where to begin? My mind was abuzz with questions. I buried my hands in my pockets and tried to make sense of it all.

"I think I understand the idea of Baby Steps: taking the creating process one step at a time," I said. "But how do you figure out which steps to take? How do you know where to start? Where do I place my focus?"

Sophia gave my arm a gentle squeeze. "I remember

so well what a jumble of questions came up when I saw how different it might be to take the Creator approach to my life. About that time I came across a wonderful passage from a letter that the great poet Rilke wrote to a younger poet he had taken under his wing."

Sophia reached into her beach bag and pulled out a journal, which appeared to be well worn. She opened the journal and looked for a particular page. "This is what Rilke said.

"Be patient toward all that is unsolved in your heart and try to love the questions themselves like locked rooms and like books that are written in a very foreign tongue. Do not now seek the answers, which cannot be given you because you would not be able to live them. And the point is to live everything. Live the questions now. Perhaps you will then gradually, without noticing it, live along some distant day into the answer."

A small sailboat bobbed out on the waves, its bright sails billowing with the sea breeze, drifting gently, serenely on the water.

"Give yourself plenty of time in coming to the answers for yourself," Sophia said warmly. "It takes time, and a lot of introspection and soul-searching, to get clear about what you really want to manifest in your life. People will begin to show up who will help you focus and sharpen your envisioned outcomes. In fact, Ted invited me to meet you so I could offer my support as you learn to live in the Creator Orientation. Others helped me to learn, and I'd be glad to help you, if you want my support."

As I took in Sophia's kind offer, I looked out at the ocean to mark the sailboat's progress. The wind was up, and the boat's sails were stretched tight and full. I wondered if such a small craft could sustain the pressure of so much force and speed. The crew scrambled about on deck, adjusting the rigging. I just hoped they knew what they were doing.

CHAPTER 7

DYNAMIC TENSION

D avid, there's another aspect of the Creator life
stance that I know Ted will want to tell you about,"
Sophia remarked. "It's the key to creating the outcomes
you'll be envisioning. Since I learned about this tool, I
use it to approach almost everything in my life."

"There's a very simple way to understand and harness
the process of creating," said Ted. "The tool Sophia's
talking about is Dynamic Tension. The way you create
any outcome in your life is to hold the vision of your
deepest desires. At the same time, though, you must
honestly and accurately assess your current situation
and how it relates to your greater vision. By doing this,
you engage a tension between what is and what can
be. This tension is the primary creative force behind
the manifestation of any outcome. It's as natural and
powerful as the force of gravity."

Sophia removed the band from her wrist and handed it to Ted with a smile. Ted turned and gave it to me. He said, "This will help you get a grip on the principle I'm talking about. Take the band and loop it around the index and middle fingers on each hand. Now stretch the band. Your right hand represents your vision and your left hand your current situation. How does that feel, David?"

"It's tight," I reported. "I can feel the tension between my hands."

"That's right. You've engaged the tension between your vision in your right hand, and your current situation in your left. Now, if that band could speak, what do you think it would say it wants to do right now?"

"It wants to relax. It wants the tension to go away."

"Right! So, here's the principle: All tension seeks to be resolved. It's not only a physical reality, as you can feel as you stretch the band, it's also a psychological principle. Human beings seek to resolve such tension all the time. If I say, "Knock, knock!" what do you want to say in response?"

"Who's there?" We all laughed.

"That's an example of resolving the tension," said Ted. "Someone says, 'Knock, knock!' and there's a tension, an expectation. You know to resolve that tension by responding, 'Who's there?' It may be a silly example, but the fact that people dislike tension and will take action to resolve it—whether consciously or unconsciously—is a powerful principle once you understand it and put it to use.

"In the case of Dynamic Tension, you can resolve the tension in either direction. You can let go of your vision (your right hand) and snap back toward your current reality, or you can move from your current situation (your left hand) toward your vision. Creators resolve the tension by taking Baby Steps to move from current reality toward their vision. When you do this, you tap into a fundamental and powerful creative principle that's hard-wired into the universe."

"This one simple idea has had a tremendous impact on the way I approach every part of my life," Sophia added. "When I decide what I want to create, it's absolutely necessary to give myself permission to dream big—not to limit my vision to what I think or know to be possible."

"But wait a minute," I said. "What if what I want to create or manifest in my life is, in fact, impossible? Don't you need to be realistic in choosing what you want to create?"

Sophia was silent for a moment. We watched as a crab burrowed into the sand a little way up the beach.

"That's an important question, one that must be considered carefully. To limit yourself to only what you know or think is possible can greatly reduce your creativity. Allow yourself to dream, David. For instance, right now, ask yourself what you would do if you knew you couldn't fail? What would you want, have, do, or become if absolutely anything were possible?"

I thought for a minute and decided to play with Sophia a bit. "I'd love to be a seven-foot center playing professional basketball," I exclaimed. "But that's not likely, given the fact that I'm a middle-aged guy well short of six feet tall."

Sophia chuckled and took the bait. "Okay, let's stay with that, David. If that's really what you want, the key is not to let go of the vision. Instead, ask yourself how you can get to the closest expression of that vision, given the reality that you will never be a seven-foot basketball player.

"So, what could you do given an accurate assessment of your current reality?" she asked. "You might join a men's basketball league and play with that vision in your mind as a fantasy expression of your desire. Maybe

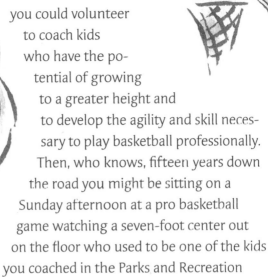

you could volunteer
to coach kids
who have the po-
tential of growing
to a greater height and
to develop the agility and skill necessary to play basketball professionally.
Then, who knows, fifteen years down
the road you might be sitting on a
Sunday afternoon at a pro basketball
game watching a seven-foot center out
on the floor who used to be one of the kids
you coached in the Parks and Recreation
League. In that case, you could say that there *was* a part
of you that did, in fact, become a seven-foot center."

Sophia went on, "Each of the Baby Steps you take
to move in the direction of your dream helps you get
clearer about the form that dream may take. While the
reality is that you will never be seven feet tall or play
professional basketball, by holding your vision and paying attention to current reality, you *can* create a way to
express that vision in a different form."

Sophia had made her point. All I could do was smile
and nod. "Got it!"

DEALING WITH ANXIETY

"Sophia gave a great example of how Dynamic Tension works—or can work," said Ted. "There's another aspect of Dynamic Tension, though. Being aware of it will allow you to consciously and effectively draw on Dynamic Tension to create your desired outcomes. Remember what we said a few minutes ago, about how the Creator Orientation is not all sweetness and light?"

"Right," I said. "It also takes a lot of hard work."

Ted nodded, "It's important to remember that anxiety and even fear are part of the human experience, and that these unpleasant emotional states very often raise their heads when we begin working creatively with Dynamic Tension. It helps to be aware that anxiety is part of the experience of manifesting. Anxiety has positive aspects, such as excitement and exhilaration, but it can also arise in ways that limit your effectiveness. In other words, you can have your anxiety but don't let your anxiety have you!"

"It took me a while to really understand the distinction between my own feelings of anxiety and the sense of Dynamic Tension—the creative force in the Creator Orientation," Sophia added. "I have a friend who really helped me understand the difference. He used to teach skydiving in the Air Force. One evening I was sharing the principle of Dynamic Tension with him, and he pointed out that the exhilaration he felt jumping out of a plane was certainly not the same thing as gravity, the force that pulled him toward the earth as he fell. The force of gravity, he told me, *contributed* to his feeling of exhilaration, but exhilaration and gravity are not the same. Likewise, the force of Dynamic Tension is not the same as the feeling of anxiety that often comes up when we tap into it."

I pondered that for a moment. I understood the distinction, but it wasn't clear to me why it was so important.

"Living and working in the Creator Orientation is a conscious process. Anxiety is like a mischievous monkey chattering its way into your thoughts. If you don't stay aware of its antics, it can quite easily propel you into the Victim Orientation," Ted said.

"How?" I asked.

"Do you remember the Inner State of the Victim Orientation that I drew in the sand yesterday?"

"It was anxiety," I recalled.

"Yes," said Ted. "And if you allow anxiety to pull you in to reacting, you'll limit the effectiveness that

Dynamic Tension offers you as you attempt to create an outcome. So, David, create the tension between your two hands with the band again. Now, if you confuse anxiety with the tension between your vision, your right hand, and your current reality, your left hand, you'll tend to react in order to release the tension, hoping it will get rid of the anxiety. Doing this may make you feel better but it will not help you create the results you want. So what is one thing you could do right now to release the tension?"

"Hmm." I looked at my hands. "Probably the easiest thing to do would be to let go of my vision." I moved my right hand toward my left.

"Absolutely! The easiest thing would be to compromise your vision. You could let go of or reduce your vision. You might convince yourself that what you want to create is unrealistic or impossible, or that you're not worthy of such a lofty dream. Then you would settle for something less than your heart's true desires. The reality, though, is that you can't invest your soul in a compromise."

Seeing my wrinkled brow, Sophia added, "Let me give you an example. About a year ago, I decided to change jobs, to move into a profession in which I could use

Ted's principles in my work. I was working as a manager
in the loan processing department of a bank, and I had
really come to dread going to work, not to mention
dealing with my difficult boss. I longed for a more
fulfilling job but couldn't afford to leave without having
a new job to take its place, so I took the first offer that
came along. I went to work as a trainer for another
company. I thought that compromise was as close as
I was going to be able to get to what I really wanted.
It ended up being the wrong move. Now I realize that
I settled for something much less than my envisioned
outcome."

"So, what did you do?" I asked.

"Well, I'm still working on resolving it. I'm still in that
job and giving it my best effort. At the same time, I'm
working with a coach to clarify my vision of what I want
my work to be. I'm giving myself the time to get really
clear before I make any more changes."

Ted nodded. "So you could compromise your vision
to resolve the tension and get rid of the anxiety you
might feel; it's the easiest, most immediate, and most
common reaction. The other way is actually much more
subtle; it has to do with how you assess your current
reality. It's all too easy not to tell the truth about your

current reality—to deny, minimize, or rationalize it away. There are many ways to shade the truth or put a certain spin on the current situation by telling yourself it's not as bad or as good as it seems."

Sophia chuckled softly. "My current job is actually the result of both those ways of reacting. Not only did I settle for something less than what I wanted, but when I was interviewed for the training position, I told myself I could probably create a coaching program once I got into the organization. I even dismissed the recruiter's comment that they considered coaching to be a function of the employee relations department rather than the training group."

"One of the keys to tapping the power of Dynamic Tension is to tell yourself the truth about your current reality," said Ted. "This is often the most challenging aspect of the process of manifesting an outcome, because people tend to see reality as either rosier or gloomier than it actually is. Telling the truth in this sense means being objective and detached enough to see reality as it is without labeling it as either good or bad."

"It's not as easy as it sounds," Sophia added. "I have a quote on my bulletin board at work to remind me of this principle. I look at it every day. The friend who gave it to me said it was from a former corporate executive. It says: 'What determines your destiny is not the hand you are dealt but how you play the hand. And the way to play the hand is to see reality for what it is and to act accordingly.' That is the challenge—to see reality for what it is."

Ted said, "Paying attention to what is true at every point along the way while you continue to hold your vision lets you make realistic decisions about which Baby Steps you will take to move yourself closer to your goal. As you move forward, you may resolve the tension by changing your situation, by modifying your vision as you get clearer about its final form, or by finding an entirely new path that will lead to your destination.

"At the same time, David, it's important to be realistic about what forward progress looks like. The way of creating is not a smooth and continuous upward curve of achievement. Some of the steps you take may end up being detours or out-and-out mistakes. By staying focused on your vision, though, you'll find even those steps useful in the creating process. There's no such thing as a wasted Baby Step.

Every step will either take you closer to or further away from what you intend to create. And that process will give you priceless information to spur you onward. If you continue applying these principles, I guarantee that you will achieve remarkable and often unpredictable results throughout your life."

"Ted is right. The Creator way of being can be quite magical," Sophia mused. "Baby Steps help us move in time from our current reality toward a vision. Many times a Baby Step is just that: an incremental act that serves your vision. But there are other times . . ." Her voice trailed off, and I noticed her eyes were moist.

"Other times," she continued, "the most amazing things happen. I call them the twin sisters: Synchronicity and Serendipity. It's when unpredictable, spontaneously helpful events appear to just happen. Something I need shows up right when I need it. I open a magazine or a book to just the right page that answers a burning question or that inspires me to take a more effective approach. Or the right person comes into my life at just the right time."

An involuntary shiver of affirmation coursed up my spine. I looked down at the Creator Orientation Ted had drawn in my journal. I looked out at the expanse of the sea, the blue waves rolling out far beyond my line of vision. I turned to Ted and Sophia, and they both smiled.

"You mean like these last two days," I said.

Sophia nodded, "It's no accident that you've come to this place and this conversation at this time in your life. Your choice to contemplate, to step into a new life stance and a new way of being, opened the door for Ted and me to meet you. Whether or not we continue to work together after today, I'm confident that we'll always be friends on the path."

"Yes, friends on the path!" smiled Ted. "And David, as you live your life from the Creator Orientation, you'll discover that your new relationships take on a much different quality than you experienced in the Victim Orientation. You now have the potential to leave the Dreaded Drama Triangle behind. In all your relationships—professional and personal—you can now step into a new framework: The Empowerment Dynamic."

CHAPTER 8

THE EMPOWERMENT DYNAMIC

The day was vibrant and the sounds of life reverberated everywhere. Gulls circled above the surf, getting into spats over which spoils belonged in whose beak. Families and couples took their places all along the beach, while a few people walked solo and were, like me, absorbed in their thoughts.

I couldn't stop thinking about this new life orientation, how I was acquiring the tools to create a more fulfilling life. I wondered what all of it might mean in the future. Whatever change lay ahead, I felt ready.

At that moment I felt someone nearby and looked over my shoulder. Ted had stood up from his perch on the rock and motioned ahead of us. "Let's walk back toward the shoreline," he said. "There's something else I want to draw in the sand for you."

The three of us strolled along the shore, Ted and me on either side of Sophia, who linked her arms in ours. It felt as though we were three old friends, surprisingly natural. In a few moments we stopped. The area seemed relatively free of sunbathers. Ted drew another triangle with the tip of his walking stick.

"The Creator Orientation challenges every assumption and attitude that the Victim Orientation holds to be true," said Ted. "A Creator puts problems in their rightful place, causing fear to fade and loosen its grip. In its place, passion, desire, even love, become your primary motivation. Though fear still comes up from time to time, the Creator stance increases your capacity to deal with anxiety in ways that actually enhance your creativity. Rather than constantly reacting to your circumstances (the Victim's way) you begin creating your experience—which means, of course, that you create a new set of relationships as well.

"These new relationships are the powerful antidote to the Victim, Persecutor, and Rescuer roles of the Dreaded Drama Triangle. By assuming the Creator Orientation, you enter a whole new set of dynamics that support rather than sabotage your happiness. It's called The Empowerment Dynamic. My nickname, Ted, comes from The Empowerment Dynamic."

"So Ted's not your real name?" I asked.

"It's my real name now!" Ted chuckled. "I don't mind sharing initials with The Empowerment Dynamic."

Sophia touched Ted's arm. "David," she turned to me, "before Ted describes this new triangle of relationships, I want to be sure of something. Do you know what an antidote is?"

"Isn't it the cure for a disease or an illness, something like that?"

"Close," Sophia smiled. "It's a remedy that counteracts the effects of a poison. TED*—The Empowerment Dynamic—counteracts the poison of DDT, the Dreaded Drama Triangle. TED* is the antidote for DDT."

Ted explained, "Each of the roles in TED* is also an antidote for its counterpart in the DDT. **Creator** is the antidote for the Victim role. The antidote for the **Persecutor** role is **Challenger** (I'll say more about that in a minute). And in The Empowerment Dynamic, support comes not from a Rescuer but from a Coach."

Ted knelt down and with his finger wrote the letters *Cr* at the top of the new triangle.

THE CREATOR ROLE

"The central role in The Empowerment Dynamic is Creator," explained Ted. "Actually, all three roles share Creator characteristics, just as all three roles in the DDT are Victim oriented.

"You could think of Creator as the light and Victim as shadow. While the Victim is powerless, a Creator claims and taps into his or her personal power in order to choose a response to life circumstances. Therein lies a Creator's power to manifest a desired outcome.

"A Creator is vision-focused and passion-motivated. To really live into your Creator self, you'll have to do the inner work necessary to find your own sense of purpose and passion—whatever touches your heart and holds meaning for you."

"Adopting a Creator stance begins simply by making a

choice. You decide and declare that in your heart, mind, and soul, you really are a Creator, not a Victim," Sophia said. "As I said before, I spent the first few months after I met Ted just making that choice every day, sensing more and more what it meant to live as a Creator. It took me some time to clarify what I wanted to create in my life. At first, all I knew was that I couldn't live as a Victim anymore. It took a while for me to learn exactly how I could step out of the Victim stance and into the Creator Orientation."

Out on the water, a surfer caught a wave and rode along as the wave crested and gradually subsided.

"It sounds almost too good to be true," I said. "I mean, living my life from a Creator Orientation is bound to be a wonderful change compared to what I've grown used to."

Sophia smiled and pointed out toward the surfer. "Living your life from a Creator perspective is kind of like what that guy's doing, like riding a wave. There will still be waves of change in your life and you will have to learn to ride them. Some of the changes will arise from your own choices and others from circumstances beyond your control. Sometimes the waves will throw you for a loop and other times you'll surf them with skill, ease, and grace. Even when the waves throw you,

you will learn from the experience and continue growing. Like a surfer whose close attention and focus can make his ride on a wave into a powerful experience of beauty and grace, by living into the Creator Orientation and The Empowerment Dynamic, in time you'll learn to navigate through life so adeptly that sometimes you'll amaze even yourself."

I watched the surfer ride the wave all the way in to the shore. He shouted with glee, shoving his fist in the air *"Yes!"* and headed back into the waves.

"You'll learn to love—or at least learn to ride—the variety of waves that life serves up," Sophia added. "You'll find yourself actually moving toward each new challenge with growing enthusiasm. Greeting your experiences as a Creator is a powerful way to live."

"A Creator has a special relationship with power," said Ted. "The kind of power that a Creator cultivates is not power over others—that is the power of the Persecutor. Instead, a Creator harnesses the power to create. Power to and power with are the dynamic duo of the Creator Orientation.

"Creators share power with others, first and foremost because they see others as Creators in their own right. Truly speaking, a Creator is actually a Co-Creator, as he or she gives in service to others while at the same time receiving support from them. Creators also receive support in ways that might seem mysterious, from unseen forces which appear to be spiritual in nature. The experiences of serendipity and synchronicity that Sophia referred to are manifestations of the unseen, but very present, Co-Creator in action.

"As a Creator enters into relationship with other Creators, together they support other people by playing the two additional roles that complete The Empowerment Dynamic: Challenger and Coach."

THE CHALLENGER ROLE

"The Challenger has many faces," Ted continued. The most common is the one who provokes others to take action. The Challenger may be compassionate or confrontational, or both. A Challenger calls forth a Creator's will to create, often spurring him or her to learn new skills, make difficult decisions, or do whatever is necessary to manifest a dream or desire. The Challenger is a kind of teacher who

points toward life's lessons, toward opportunities for growth embedded in the living of life.

"Like the relationship of Persecutor to Victim, the Challenger to a Creator is usually a person, but it may also be a condition or circumstance. All of life's experiences are teachers in some sense, challenging us to grow and evolve. Although the Persecutor certainly provokes a reaction, the Challenger elicits a response by encouraging a Creator to acquire new knowledge, skill, or insight. Both roles initiate change, but in different ways."

Ted bent over and scratched *Ch* in the sand at one corner of the triangle.

Sophia said, "I once worked for a manager who was one of the most difficult people I ever knew. She pushed all my emotional buttons. But as I look back on the experience of working with her, I realize how much I learned. I learned how not to treat others, for one thing. Being in that situation also forced me to clarify the work I really wanted to do, and to learn to stay centered in the face of what I could have easily called one tough Persecutor."

Ted smiled. "I remember, Sophia, how you were struggling with your manager at that time. The Challengers who come into your life, David, may be either constructive or deconstructive in nature. Constructive Challengers spark improvement or development of some kind. They coax, cajole, and entice you to move in the directions of your heart's desires. This kind of Challenger is a teacher who challenges your pet notions, your view of the status quo. Most of the time, constructive Challengers are aware of what they are doing when they challenge you. They see you as a Creator, and they encourage your learning, growth, and development.

"Deconstructive Challengers, on the other hand, cause you to take apart your experience in order to learn from it. These teachers may be unwelcome people, conditions, or circumstances, such as a relationship that teaches you to face something difficult in yourself, especially something that is inhibiting your capacity to create. Sophia's manager was one of these for her. A deconstructive Challenger might be an event that wakes you up to possibilities or to problems for which you can discover a creative solution.

"Even this kind of Challenger bestows a great gift, although it rarely feels that way. The gift is usually one of clarity—showing you what you want or don't want, what you need to leave behind, or what you must learn so that you don't repeat a painful experience."

Sophia turned to me with compassion in her eyes, and I felt the question coming. "Who or what have been your Challengers, David?"

I sifted through my woes for a moment. My dad's death, my infertility, and my ex-wife's emotional withdrawal—all were Challengers, without a doubt.

"When my dad passed away, it challenged me to develop my sense of myself as an adult." I was thinking out loud. "He used to challenge me to consider the impact I was making. He taught me to always ask myself whether I was leaving other people or situations better off than I found them. That was his personal measure of success, and when he died I adopted that measure within myself more completely. I can see the example he set for me and how his death was a constructive Challenger in my life.

"My infertility is a little trickier, though. It certainly has been a deconstructive Challenger. It made me take stock of a lot of things, especially how I see my contribution in the world. Not being able to father my own children is a deep loss, but I also know there are plenty of opportunities to father children in the role of stepfather or adoptive parent, or to volunteer with a community service organization as a mentor to young people. Lately, I've also realized that my larger contribution may have more to do with what I offer through my work.

"My ex-wife was also a deconstructive Challenger. Her withdrawal from our marriage, which I can now see with a bit more compassion, made me think about what I really wanted in a relationship. I know that I want a healthy relationship, but I'm not entirely sure what that looks like. I have so much to learn and explore before I'm ready to open up to a new intimate relationship."

Sophia smiled kindly. "David, you're already doing the work of a Creator. To be able to look on those experiences in which you've seen yourself as a Victim, to see them now as Challengers that have taught you something—that's one giant step! It's one of the major shifts in awareness that TED* brings. Already you're transforming your relationship to your life experiences."

"Seeing that you have much to learn and to explore brings us to the third role in The Empowerment Dynamic: the Coach," remarked Ted.

THE COACH ROLE

As he wrote *Co* in the lower right corner of his sand drawing, Ted asked, "What comes to mind when you think about a coach, David?"

"I think of sports . . . maybe a football coach or a basketball coach," I said.

"The role of Coach in The Empowerment Dynamic is a bit different. In the sports world, a coach doesn't actively engage in the field of play. The coach is on the sidelines, strategizing and helping to coordinate the individual efforts of the team members, with the goal of winning the game. A good sports coach helps his or her players believe they can win—or at least play their best—by guiding them to develop the skills and attitudes that lead to success.

"A Coach in The Empowerment Dynamic shares that characteristic of encouragement with a sports coach. But there is at least one key difference between a typical sports coach and a Coach in The Empowerment Dynamic.

"A TED* Coach is fully engaged in the field of play— the Creator Orientation—in his or her own life. First and foremost, a Coach knows he or she is a Creator, and sees other people as Creators as well.

"The Coach is the antidote to the Victim's Rescuer in the DDT. While both Coach and Rescuer seek to support the other person (the Victim or Creator), the Rescuer actually draws power away from the Victim and reinforces his or her powerlessness. A Coach leaves the power with the Creator and seeks only to help facilitate her personal progress. A Coach is the embodiment of a Creator's desire to share power with another."

Sophia looked at Ted and playfully signaled *time out*. "Hang on, Coach! David, let me share some of my experience in working with several different types of Coaches. I've been blessed to have a number of great Coaches, including this guy here."

Sophia and Ted caught each others' eyes and chuckled. Their lightness lifted my spirits.

"When Dan and I were first breaking up, I worked with a dynamite therapist and licensed social worker. She asked a lot of good questions that helped me probe into my past so I could begin to understand the sources of some of the patterns of behavior that had contributed to our relationship's breakdown. Then she helped me begin to release them and replace the old behaviors with more functional ways of being in relationship.

"I was working with her when I first met Ted. Just as he is sharing with you, he helped me open to a whole different way of thinking and to see that I could create a future that was not bound by my past. As a result of my conversations with Ted, I decided to begin working with a certified coach, who helped me clarify what I wanted and to develop strategies for creating outcomes. All three—the therapist, Ted, and the certified coach—acted as Coaches for me because they supported my own exploration."

Ted added, "A Coach in The Empowerment Dynamic doesn't necessarily need to be professionally trained, such as the therapist and professional coach Sophia worked with. A Coach can simply be a trusted friend, which I know I have been for Sophia. It is true, however, that there are times when it may be important to work with a professional.

"A Coach supports, assists, and facilitates a Creator in manifesting a desired outcome. A Coach holds others to be whole, resourceful, and creative. Coaches don't regard those who turn to them for support as somehow broken or in need of fixing, which is the Rescuer's viewpoint. Instead, a Coach helps others see new possibilities, helps them to dare to dream."

"That's right," Sophia chimed in. "A Coach is a source of knowledge, but he doesn't tell a Creator what she should or shouldn't do. Instead, he asks a lot of good questions and listens deeply to what a Creator is saying as she thinks, probes, and explores. A Coach is constantly alert to possibility. My Coaches are able to see possibilities that may be invisible to me; they help ignite my inspiration, and they're committed to my success as I forge my own way in life. They say, 'I'm going to stand beside you, no matter what,' and they mean it. What they don't say, though, is 'Here, let me fix it for you," or—even more importantly—'Let me fix YOU!' which is the approach of the Rescuer.

"When I began working with a professional coach, he shared the definition of a couch from the International Coach Federation." Sophia opened her journal again, found the page she was looking for, and handed it to me. I read the definition she had written:

> Professional coaches provide an ongoing partner-
> ship designed to help clients produce fulfilling
> results in their personal and professional lives.
> Coaches help people improve their performances
> and enhance the quality of their lives. Coaches are
> trained to listen, to observe, and to customize their
> approach to individual client needs. They seek to
> elicit solutions and strategies from the client; they
> believe the client is naturally creative and resource-
> ful. The coach's job is to provide support to enhance
> the skills, resources, and creativity that the client
> already has.

"Having that kind of support must be awesome," I said. "I've worked with a therapist before—that's how I found out about Karpman's Drama Triangle. And I can see how she acted as a Coach, of sorts, in the way she helped me explore. But if you are not professionally trained, how does a Coach go about working with a Creator?"

Sophia reached over and pulled the exercise band out of Ted's pocket. She stretched it between her two hands the way I had done earlier. "One really effective way is to use Dynamic Tension. You can be a Coach for others by asking them questions that help them gain clarity about what they want to create in life. Help them assess their current reality—both what is helpful in creating their vision and what is inhibiting and getting in the way. Then explore with them possible Baby Steps they can commit to. That will begin to bring their heart's desires into reality. The main thing is to remember to see the other as a

Creator, to be curious and ask good questions to help them clarify, to listen and support them in their own self-discovery process."

"A Coach cultivates empowerment and hope in the heart of a Creator," Ted pointed out. "For the most part, a Coach is forward and future focused, supporting a Creator to learn from the past and from current realities. From time to time, a good Coach will consciously assume the role of constructive Challenger. Ultimately, a Coach helps a Creator take ownership and assume personal power, so he or she can respond consciously and purposefully to life's circumstances. With the help of a Coach, a Creator can stay centered in the Creator Orientation. Staying centered allows you to become much more effective in the outer world, since you can focus on your envisioned outcomes and choose your response to whatever comes up—whether it is easy or challenging."

"It really sounds too good to be true," I said.

"As we've said," Sophia responded, "TED* isn't all sweetness and light. Even in this way of being, we can feel the weight of circumstances and lose sight of what's most important to us. Those are the times when we most need a Coach. We all face problems and challenges that test our strength, but as we face and find our way through them, we grow in fortitude, wisdom, and compassion—and these gifts we can share with others. Tough times are the fire in which our Creator character is made strong and whole."

I looked at Sophia, then over at Ted, then at Ted's triangle in the sand. I felt almost light-headed as I considered the possibility of actually living this way. What would my life look like, centered in a position of empowerment, with the support of great Coaches to help me understand and respond creatively to my Challengers?

I looked out at the sea, and then up the shore toward the bench where Ted and I had met. Far out on the water the little sailboat had made its way up the coast. The seagulls, the surfers, and the sunbathers continued up and down the beach, while the crashing of the waves surrounded us.

"I sure would prefer to live my life as a Creator. I'm tired of wallowing in the DDT. It looks so easy on paper—or on the sand. But I have so many years of practice and habit living out the Dreaded Drama Triangle. I know all three of those roles forward and backward. How do I make the shift from DDT to TED*?"

"*Aahhh*," said Ted, "that's an important question, David. Let's explore how Shift Happens!"

CHAPTER 9

Shift Happens

"Maybe you've heard this before," remarked Ted. "You're not a human being seeking a spiritual experience; you're a spiritual being having a human experience. It's true. All human beings are spiritual beings, but most sleepwalk through their days. They are unaware of the reality that they have a greater capacity for choice than they know.

"The vicious cycle created by the Victim Orientation and the Dreaded Drama Triangle pulls people into the darkest depths of the human experience and breeds hopelessness. They long for a magical someone or something to race to their rescue. But no matter how much tough luck the human experience dishes out, the Creator Orientation and The Empowerment Dynamic provide a larger perspective. This is what I mean about your taking on a spiritual perspective. Instead of a vicious cycle of reacting, this perspective offers a virtuous cycle of growth and development to anyone who adopts it. Think of it this way, David. Your life is a kind of learning laboratory where you're constantly experimenting with your own higher knowing, always increasing your capacity to design your life and to choose your response to what happens to you.

"Human beings must create; it's hard-wired. The reality is this: you cannot *not* create! The question is, are you creating consciously or sleepwalking through your life, simply reacting to what comes at you?

"While you may not directly cause everything that happens to you, you do have the capacity to choose your response to circumstances. And you have a great deal more responsibility for what appears in your life than you might want to admit. One of the biggest challenges is waking up to this reality, making the shift happen on a daily basis, and working to stay awake."

"That reminds me of Victor Frankl," Sophia said. "He was a psychologist who was imprisoned in Nazi death camps during World War II. He lived through unspeakable hardships and could easily have qualified as a Victim. During that time, though, Victor Frankl had a mind-blowing revelation. I have a quote from him written in my journal here. 'Everything can be taken from a (person) but one thing: the last of the human freedoms—to choose one's attitude in any given set of circumstances, to choose one's own way.' To me, that's quite a Creator statement!"

I looked out at the ocean. "I have to say, all this feels a little overwhelming. It's a lot to take in, and to take on."

Sophia replied, "I know, David. When Ted and I first had this conversation, I felt the strangest mixture of excitement and fear. Right now you're setting a new course. It's going to affect the rest of your life, so take it easy. Take it a day at a time. The journey starts with the fundamental choice to live from the Creator Orientation."

Sophia's description fit perfectly. In the pit of my stomach a weird cocktail of emotions was shaking itself up.

"Try using your own Dynamic Tension—those mixed emotions—by consciously choosing to live as a Creator," she continued. "Each day, take a look at your current reality. When and where do the old habits of the Victim Orientation show up? Likewise, what's it like when you're in alignment with the Creator Orientation? Pay attention to these new choices and behaviors, and celebrate them! Keep on taking the Baby Steps that will transform the reactivity of the DDT and Victimhood into your new way of being."

"You make it sound so easy," I said.

"As I said before, it's simple but not always easy," Sophia said. "It's important to develop the habit of noticing the choices you are making. I spend about twenty minutes each morning doing this. I sit quietly and say a little prayer of gratitude for my awakening. Then I invite guidance to support my living more fully as a Creator. I end by affirming that I choose to live this way, cultivating TED* relationships that offer mutual support. I spend a few minutes remembering how I did the day before in moving toward Creator choices. Then I decide on three Baby Step actions I will take that day. They're usually things like having a particular conversation or reading an article or making an appointment. It's amazing how those Baby Steps give momentum and purpose to my day.

"There are two important criteria for defining a Baby Step. First, it is something that is doable—something I can really take action on. The second is that it is 100 percent mine to do. That second one really makes me stop sometimes because it forces me to clarify my own responsibility and the fact that I can't make someone else take a step for me. Doable and 100 percent mine to do—remember these principles as you choose your own Baby Steps."

"In the end, David, we're talking about choice," Ted pointed out. "On the one hand, it is about choosing what you feel called to create and the steps you take in the process of living into your vision. On the other

20 MINUTES A DAY
• sit quietly - gratitude
• invite guidance
• affirm orientation (TED*)
• review yesterday's choices
• decide on 3 baby steps for today
1 _____
2 _____
3 _____

hand, you also choose your response to what shows up in your life—either as a conscious response or an unconscious reaction. When you simply react, it means you are choosing the way of the Victim. If, on the other hand, you stay mindful of current reality and determine how best to respond, you've entered The Empowerment Dynamic."

Sophia added, "Unfortunately, before they can begin to make better choices, most people have to hit bottom in the Victim Orientation and the dynamics of the DDT. Some people say that insanity is doing the same thing over and over again, hoping for different results. As that way of being gets more painful, the possibility of breaking through to the Creator Orientation and TED* opens up. Then, just as it is happening with you, a person reaches that sacred and bittersweet place called the Choice Point."

"What do you mean by Choice Point?" I asked.

Ted's eyes sparkled. "As you go through your daily experience, at every point in time you are faced with a choice about which Orientation and dynamic you want to live within, and which role you're going to play. The Choice Point is that moment in which you can consciously make a shift happen. The main way you make

the shift is by choosing a more empowered role to play.
Consider the roles within the DDT and TED* relationship triangles. You can shift roles to shift Orientations."

Ted reached out with his walking stick and drew a
vertical line in the sand. At the top he scratched *Cr*, and
at the bottom he wrote the letter *V*.

VICTIM ▶ CREATOR

"There are two ways to look at the shift between roles,"
Ted said. "First, you can change the way you see yourself; that very choice begins to make the shift happen.
Second, you can change the way you view the people,
conditions, and circumstances in your life; this also creates a shift.

"You might call one shift **intrapersonal**, meaning
within yourself. This is where you shift how you meet
your life experience. The other shift is **interpersonal**,
which involves how you interact with others. This
means being conscious of the roles you play in relating
to and with others. As you focus on making shift happen, there is one reality that you must always keep in
mind: you can only change yourself. You cannot make
shift happen for others. However, as you grow more
skilled at taking on the roles of Creator, Challenger, and

Coach, others may make their own choices to change—but you cannot make it your goal to change them. You can only change yourself."

"You've already made the most important shift, David," Sophia said. "But let me ask you this. When you find yourself lapsing into the Victim role from time to time, how do you think you could make the shift to Creator?"

I thought over all that Ted and Sophia had told me about Creator Orientation. "Well," I said, "I could remember that a Creator stays focused on a desired outcome, while a Victim is focused on problems. I guess the first thing I'd have to do would be to decide what I really want."

"You're a pretty quick study!" Sophia gave me a big grin. "That's the key to making the shift happen. You stop and ask yourself: What do I really want here? If I could have or do or be anything my heart desired right now, what would that look like? Who and how do I choose to be in this situation?

"Just asking the question shifts your focus toward what you want to create. And there's one other very important thing to consider. When you're asking what you want, make sure that whatever it is, it's intended for the highest good and won't bring harm to anyone or anything."

"Okay," I said. "But isn't being a Creator about manifesting whatever you want?"

"Well, yes and no," Sophia smiled. "Yes, because it is about creating what you want to bring into your life. But no, a Creator doesn't focus only on what he or she wants without considering its impact on others. Creating in that way would be ego-driven. Insisting on that kind of creating can easily set you up for slipping into the Persecutor role, losing touch with the Creator stance."

Ted explained, "Asking yourself what you want—rather than focusing on what you don't want—is the way of making shift happen between both the Victim and Creator orientations and Victim and Creator roles. It is choosing what you want to create, keeping in mind what Sophia just said, and it is choosing your response to your current realities. That is the intrapersonal shift.

"Standing in the position of Creator carries with it a great deal of responsibility, including how you respond to others, which is the interpersonal shift. Most of humanity is still sleepwalking through life in the Victim Orientation. You can help nudge people awake, depending on how you interact with them. But you cannot force them to make any of the shifts we are talking about."

Sophia interjected, "I've learned that one the hard way, Ted. I finally figured out that the fastest way of getting someone to see me as a Persecutor is for me to tell them that they are just being a Victim."

Ted smiled and nodded in agreement. "First and foremost, a Creator extends compassion to others. You can do this by seeing people as being Creators, whether they know it or not, and whether they are acting like it or not. As you make this shift in the way you see and interact with others, you can consciously step into one of the other TED* roles. You become a Co-Creator by serving as either a Challenger or a Coach, depending on the situation."

PERSECUTOR ▸ CHALLENGER

Ted placed his stick just below the *Cr* and drew a diagonal line that ended just to the left of the *V*. He wrote *P* at the top and *Ch* at the bottom. He said, "This is one of the most powerful shifts of all: from Persecutor to Challenger. Most Persecutors show up in your life as deconstructive Challengers; you'd rather avoid them. But when you're able to shift your view of persecuting people, conditions, or circumstances, the strangest thing happens—their actions have an entirely different impact on you: the empowering impact of the Challenger. Discovering this opens up a whole new world of possibility.

"You may wake up to a greater understanding of your anger, for one thing. Anger is one of the most powerful and feared of human emotions. In the DDT, anger correlates with fear: it's the central emotion of the Persecutor. With TED*, though, anger can be a powerful motivating force. Used constructively, it helps you to move toward whatever you're passionate about."

"I'm not sure what you mean," I said

"Behind every experience of anger lies something you care about—otherwise you wouldn't feel the anger," explained Ted. "Many great contributions arose as empowered responses to anger. Gandhi, for example, felt anger about the injustice of British rule over India. It fueled his determination to lead a peaceful resistance movement that led India's people to win their independence.

"Another possibility presented by The Empowerment Dynamic is forgiveness. You cannot make the shift from Persecutor to Challenger without some measure of forgiveness, of both yourself and others. Someone once said that forgiveness is giving up the hope of ever having a better past. There's nothing you can do to change the past, but you can choose how you think about what has already happened in your life. You then apply the learning from that experience to the process of creating what you care about."

"Anger and forgiveness were so important in my learning from and letting go of my relationship with Dan," Sophia said. "At one point I came across a quote from the writer and philosopher Henri Nouwen, who said, 'Forgiveness changes the way we remember. It converts the curse into a blessing.' Once I surrendered to the fact that I could not change what had already happened between Dan and me, I was able to redirect my energy to focus on what I wanted to create in my life. Now I can honestly say I'm grateful for our divorce, painful as it was, because of what I've learned and overcome by dealing with it."

"When problems and obstacles arise—and they always do—they're part of the creating process," said Ted. "Welcome them as teachers that are challenging you to grow. In this way, you transform your situation into an opportunity for action or at least for learning, and the gift of the Challenger is yours. The pain received from the Persecutor then magically becomes the bittersweet fruit of deepening knowledge, of learning from your experience."

I thought about how anger and forgiveness had been darting around inside me in various ways in response to Dad's passing, the infertility, and the divorce. It felt like sifting through the rubble of what seemed to be the ruins of my life.

"So how do I begin to do that?" I asked.

"There's an exercise you can use," Sophia offered. "First make a list of the people, conditions, or circumstances you have thought of as Persecutors. For each one of them, list at least seven ways they have been a gift or a teacher to you. How have they challenged you to learn and grow?"

I groaned. "With some things that's easier said than done!"

"Maybe so," Sophia said. "But I think you'll be surprised at what you uncover. The trick is to keep asking yourself questions: What is the lesson this person or situation is bringing into my life? How and what can I learn from this? What's the gift hidden in this situation, no matter how difficult it appears?

"Once you've written down the Challenger's lessons and gifts, spend some time going a little deeper. I suggest journaling at that point. As things become clearer, ask yourself more questions: What insights have I gained from this experience? Is this lesson complete for now? If it is, am I fully ready to forgive, let go, and move forward in my life? By making this list and asking these questions, you can transform all your Persecutors into Challengers!"

"David," said Ted, "there's another aspect of making the shift from Persecutor to Challenger that can be even trickier than what Sophia's describing."

"What could be trickier than that?" I blurted.

"What we've been talking about so far is the intrapersonal shift—how you choose to respond to a Persecutor in your life. The trickier shift is the interpersonal one, when you find yourself in the role of Persecutor or if someone perceives you as one. Shifting yourself from Persecutor to Challenger takes tremendous conscious focus and effort—and no small measure of humility. You can often tell if someone is perceiving you as a Persecutor by the way he reacts to what you say or do. If he starts getting defensive, that's a clue that you are showing up for him in the Persecutor role."

I thought back to my experience with my ex-wife as our marriage was crumbling. There were so many times when she reacted defensively to what I said or did.

There could be no doubt that I had repeatedly fallen into the Persecutor role.

Ted continued, "When you notice how the other person is reacting to you, the first thing to do is to clarify your intention. What are you really doing? If your intention is to look good, to be right, to be one up, or to instill fear, then you must stop in your tracks. Gather yourself and apologize for your actions or words. Then, the hardest part is to let go of the whole thing.

"One the other hand, if you are clear that your intention is to challenge the other person to learn or to develop his capacity as a Creator, the best thing to do is to ask for a 'do over.' Begin by acknowledging that your behavior did not come across as you had intended and apologize. This communication closes the gap between your intention and the negative impact of your previous approach. When you're making the interpersonal shift from Persecutor to Challenger, it's important to acknowledge the other person's worth, his power, and his responsibility for making his own choices and decisions. Then you can invite him to consider your point of view. The challenge is to adopt a take-it-or-leave-it stance about whatever you share or suggest. The decision to take your advice is his to make. Everyone creates his or her own life experience and has a set of personal lessons to learn. The choices people make will create the outcomes they reap."

"I call it the Challenger challenge," Sophia said, "because it is the most difficult TED* role to master. Becoming a conscious and constructive Challenger takes a lot of time to develop."

Sophia then took a step toward me. "David, if your former wife were standing here with us, what could you say to her to make the shift from Persecutor to Challenger?"

A flock of pelicans soared along the edge of the bluff and down the beach. As I thought about what I might say, I felt my heart loosen and, with that, a flood of tears. I choked out a few words. "I'd say I was sorry for the way I blamed and verbally attacked her. I'd tell her I know she was going through a difficult time, too. And I'd want her to know that I believe she was doing the best she could . . . in her own way."

"Excellent," Sophia said. "Now what would you say your intention was?"

"Strange," I said. "My intention was to connect with her, to bridge the distance between us. But the things I did actually drove us further apart. I'd tell her that. I'd tell her how I want to learn and grow through this process even though it's painful, and that I want to keep communicating, wherever it leads us. Then I'd ask if she was willing to talk it over."

"Good start," Sophia said. "What would you do if she said no to talking?"

"Well, instead of feeling rejected and reacting as a Victim, I'd like to believe that, if I was really speaking in the framework of TED*, I'd accept that as her choice. I'd just leave her with an open invitation to talk when and if she was ready."

"And that, my dear, is the way of a Creator." Sophia grinned. "And while it may be easier said than done, that's the way it is said and that's the way it is done. It *is* possible!"

Ted, who had been listening attentively, now chimed in. "I must say, it's fun to see you two working together. Keep in mind, too, that a Creator is capable of consciously assuming either the role of Challenger or the role of Coach."

RESCUER ▸ COACH

Ted drew a third line in the sand. At the top end of this line he wrote *R*, and at the bottom, *Co*. He then turned to me and said, "One of the biggest temptations of people who want to help others, to make a contribution in the world, is to fall into the Victim Orientation role of Rescuer. It's one thing to lend a helping hand when someone has fallen, but it's quite another to assume you have to walk on his or her behalf. A Rescuer sees the other person as a needy and powerless Victim. Rescuers breed dependence; they thrive on the need to be needed by a Victim.

"A Coach, on the other hand, remembers that other people are creative, resourceful whole beings, capable of creating their heart's desires—again, whether they know it or not and whether they act like it or not. A Coach assumes others are responsible for their life choices and experiences.

"A Rescuer is attached to outcomes and sees it as his responsibility to fix the Victim, but a Coach is not attached to any particular outcome. Rather, the Coach serves and supports a Creator in manifesting his or her desired outcomes.

"On the intrapersonal level, if you perceive that someone is trying to be a Rescuer or to fix you or your situation, the way to make shift happen is to thank them for their concern and to own your responsibility as a Creator. You can then invite them to help you as a Coach, if it feels right."

I asked, "So what can I do when I want to help someone without becoming a Rescuer myself? It's so easy for me to take on that role."

"Be curious. Ask questions," answered Sophia. "A Coach's major contribution is in the questions he asks. Rescuers have a tendency to tell others what they should do, giving advice or instruction. Coaches make occasional suggestions, but without concerning themselves with whether other people follow their recommendations. Great Coaches ask great questions that help Creators gain clarity about what they want. Questions also help Creators accurately assess their current reality, decide what needs to be done, and commit to the actions that support them in moving toward fulfilling their dreams."

"When we were exploring the nature of the Victim yesterday, you might remember that every Victim has a dream that somehow has been denied or thwarted," said Ted.

"One of the most powerful and helpful ways to shift from Rescuer to Coach is to ask the other person what it is that *she* wants," Sophia added. "Help her identify the dream that has been denied or thwarted. What do you really want here? If you could have or do or be anything your heart desired right now, what would that look like? Who and how do you choose to be or to respond in this situation? These are all questions that help a person shift into her own Creator Orientation.

"Another great way to contribute is to help someone see the gifts and lessons a Persecutor has made available to them," Sophia continued. "You can do that by asking her the same sort of questions I raised a minute ago when you were working to make your own shift from the Persecutor to the Challenger role. You might ask: What is the lesson this person or situation is bringing into your life? How and what can you learn from this? What's the gift hidden in this situation, no matter how difficult it appears?"

The sun was beginning its slow descent toward the horizon. Our shadows encircled Ted's sand drawing, which now looked something like an asterisk.

As I studied the crossroads in the sand, I felt Ted's hand on my shoulder.

"There you have it, David. All your choices are right here at your feet. Here you can see all the roles of the Victim Orientation, with its Dreaded Drama Triangle, as well as the Creator Orientation and The Empowerment Dynamic. My challenge to you, my friend, is to stay awake to the choices you make every day and to the relationships you cultivate."

Then Ted pulled something from his shirt pocket: a small pendant of some sort, strung on brown twine. As Ted held it out, I saw that it was in the shape of a tiny sand dollar.

"This is for you, David. It's to remind you of all you now know. In this way it offers a source of protection. See the center? It's an asterisk like the one in the sand, a symbol of the choice you always have before you: Victim or Creator."

Ted looked at me for a long moment before reaching over my head and placing the amulet around my neck.

CHAPTER 10

A FOND FAREWELL

Stunned, I looked down at the pendant. In the late afternoon light, the small reminder glowed slightly against my shirt. Just then Sophia pulled a similar pendant from her sweatshirt and held it up for me to see. My heart felt suddenly larger, as if it were expanding to contain the moment. The two of them had given me so much: their wisdom, their experience, their close attention. They had come near when everyone and everything else in my life seemed to have fallen away. Ted and Sophia had listened and offered a new perspective. Most of all, they had helped point a way forward for my life when I had felt so stuck. They had laughed with me and cared. I looked up at the sky. Such friends. Such sky! Something else inside let go just then. Like a prisoner stepping into the light of freedom, I let the tears flow.

"Emotions are a measure of how important some-thing is to you, David," said Ted. "I'm happy to welcome your tears of release. I trust you'll take what you've learned these past two days and continue growing in that new knowledge. You seem to have found what you were searching for when you came to the beach."

"I found more than I can say. Much more."

My mind was whirling, imagining all the ways that I could begin applying TED* in my life. The sunshine felt warmer, the sounds of the shore were filled with meaning. Sacred moments passed. I stammered, "I can already think of so many people and places where TED* can make things better; not only in my own life, but for other people, too. I want to practice what I've learned here with my associates at work. I want to share it with these newlyweds I know and . . . and my sister's family—in fact, everybody's family. Boy, I wish I had known about this way of being while I was growing up. I'll bet young people would really appreciate TED*'s help. There are so many areas this could apply to—the possibilities are endless."

Ted laughed. "Hang on, David! Slow down a bit. It's true, there's not a single aspect of the human experience to which TED*—The Empowerment

Dynamic—does not apply. Take it a step at a time and one aspect of your life at a time. Eventually, you will find that much of your life has been influenced by TED*. But those explorations must wait for another day. The sun will be going down soon, and it's time to call it a day."

"David," Sophia said, "I'd love to stay in touch and be of support in whatever ways I can—as a friend, as a Coach, and maybe from time to time as a Challenger. Your personal growth will be my reward. It's no accident that Ted brought us together. We've been down similar paths and I know there are things we can learn from each other."

"That would be great, Sophia. Thanks," I said. I saw that Ted had closed his eyes. Sophia did the same, so I followed suit.

"Let's be silent for a moment," said Ted, "I want to express my gratitude for our meeting, and for this work and way of being that has been entrusted to us. Let the sounds outside wash over us."

And so I did. I gave thanks for all that had happened, for my new connections and the new sense of hope that was now coursing through me. I drank in the sounds of the waves, breathed in the smell of the ocean, and let the warmth of the day sink in.

After a few minutes someone gave my hand a squeeze and I opened my eyes. It was Ted. He had taken both my hand and Sophia's. He looked deeply at her and then at me. I felt a little funny then, as if Ted were looking into and beyond me. It reminded me of the way my dad looked at me when I graduated from college. I had known then that he saw exactly what I was made of, that he loved me for all that I was and even for all that I wasn't. I smiled back.

"Until next time." Ted gave us both a hug. Such a warm soul! I felt like my heart might bubble over.

Sophia turned, grabbed my hands, and gave me an exuberant squeeze as if she were a long lost sister returning home. I closed my eyes and relaxed into the moment. What a blessing to feel this way, I thought to myself. After a long minute, I opened my eyes and turned to Ted.

And Ted wasn't there. He was sauntering down the shore, his walking stick making little marks in the sand. They looked like little periods, punctuating the end of this two-day conversation. He turned back to us, grinned, and waved goodbye.

Sophia laughed. "He has a way of doing that! One thing I can predict: this won't be the last time you see

Ted." She reached out and touched my pendant. I liked having it there, resting over my heart.

We stood for a few minutes looking out at the waves together and then Sophia said, "Well, time to head home." We said our goodbyes. As Sophia was leaving, she called out over her shoulder, "I'll e-mail you after dinner!"

Walking up the beach toward the car, I took my time. There was the bluff and the path where Ted and I had made our way down here both yesterday and today. The sun had dipped lower now, and the clouds had taken on a pink glow. Scanning the top of the bluff, I could just make out the bench where I had first come to sit and think and write in my journal. How different I felt now.

"Thank you, Ted, for introducing me to TED* (The Empowerment Dynamic)," I said aloud, smiling. "Thank you very much."

A Note
from the Author

Writers write what they most need to learn. At least this writer does! During the writing of this book I was presented with many opportunities to cast off Victimhood, reconsidering and applying TED* (The Empowerment Dynamic) in new and exciting ways. My personal and professional life constantly urges me to observe and understand the human experience more deeply. As a teacher, facilitator, coach, and consultant, my passion has long been to help improve people's individual and collective capacity for living and working together. As I live out this passion, I've come to realize that the most fundamental relationship—the one at the heart of all others—is the relationship to ourselves and our life experience.

Each day I awaken to a range of choices that will shape my reality and my life. Some days are better than others. Like the weather outside my window, some mornings bring sun and clarity; others seem dusted with a grey haze. Like Sophia, I'm still living my way into what it means to be rooted in the Creator Orientation.

So I try to stay alert, ready to welcome the Challengers and Coaches that make life a rich learning experience.

This little book is part autobiography and part fiction. Which parts are which is, in the end, of no real consequence. The really important questions are these: Where do you see *yourself* in the story? What kinds of choices are *you* making? And what is the Baby Step that will make a shift happen in your life, *today*?

May we individually live into our own answers while seeing all those around us as the Creators they actually are. By offering our gifts to others as Coaches and constructive Challengers, we can create a world that works for all of us. For, ultimately, that is the true power of TED*.

QUESTIONS
FOR THE JOURNEY

Check Your Compass

In the book, Ted introduces David to the Victim Orientation and then later encourages him to adopt a Creator Orientation.

- Reflect on the times when you know you are (or have been) in the Victim Orientation. What kinds of people or situations do you focus on that can trigger you to "go reactive?" What emotions (inner state) arise during those times?

- When you are in the Victim Orientation, do you tend to react in a flight, fight or freeze, mannner? What do you do?

- What attracts you to the idea of adopting a Creator Orientation for your life and work?

- What practices can you put into place to consciously focus on what you want on a daily basis?

- Reflect on a time in your life when you were passionate about an outcome you created? How did "passion" feel in that experience? How did you deal with problems when they arose?

- How might you catch yourself and shift from a Victim to a Creator Orientation?

Dance of Relationship Dynamics

The Victim Orientation produces and perpetuates the Dreaded Drama Triangle (DDT)™, while adopting and moving into a Creator Orientation fosters TED* (*The Empowerment Dynamic) ™. Learning to "make the shift" from the DDT to TED* is the key to a more resourceful, resilient and fulfilling way to relate to others, your experience, and yourself.

- How do you know when you are in the DDT? What is your experience and how does it feel?

- How do you behave when you are in the Victim role?

- How do you act when you are in the Persecutor role?

- What do you do when you are in the Rescuer role?

- Which of the DDT roles do you most commonly take on?

- Which of the TED* roles are you most attracted to: Creator, Challenger, or Coach?

- Which of the TED* roles do you find the most challenging?

- What might you do to shift from the Victim to the Creator role?

- What might you do to shift from the Persecutor to Challenger role?

- What might you do to shift form the Rescuer to the Coach role?

- Who are some people from your life—or from history—that are inspiring examples of Creators? What is it about them that moves you and that you would like to emulate?

Ready, Set, Go

Creating outcomes requires harnessing Dynamic Tension and taking Baby Steps toward what has heart and meaning—including the solving of problems.

- What would you create if you knew you could not fail? How do you describe what you want to create as an outcome?

- Telling the truth about current reality is important. When you "shade" current reality, do you tend to see things as "rosier" or "gloomier" than they really are?

- When you are struggling to "hold the tension" between your vision and current reality, do you more often feel drawn to compromise your vision or not tell the truth about current reality?

- What appeals to you about the concept of Baby Steps?
- When have you taken a Baby Step that ended up being a breakthrough or a "quantum leap?"

APPENDIX

A Synopsis of *The Power of TED**
(*The Empowerment Dynamic)

This section provides an overview of the frameworks and key concepts from *The Power of TED**, in the same order in which they appear in the fable.

The Dreaded Drama Triangle (DDT): Victim, Persecutor, Rescuer--Based on Stephen Karpman's original Drama Triangle, the DDT involves three intertwined roles.

1. Victim. The central figure in the DDT, a Victim is one who feels powerless and has experienced some loss, thwarted desire or aspiration, and/or the psychic death of a dream. An important distinction is made between *victimhood*, which is a situation in which one is victimized to some degree, and *Victimhood*, which is a self-identity and "poor me" life stance.

2. Persecutor. The Persecutor serves as the cause of the Victim's perceived powerlessness, reinforcing the Victim's "Poor Me" identity. The Persecutor may be a person, condition (such as a health condition), or a circumstance (a natural disaster, for example). When the Persecutor is a person, he or she is symbiotically linked to the Victim and seeks to dominate (either overtly or covertly) and maintain a "one-up"

position through a variety of assertive and/or manipulative means. Often a Persecutor's behavior is driven by his own fear of becoming, or re-becoming, a Victim. Fear of losing control can also be a factor.

3. Rescuer. The Rescuer is any person or activity (such as an addiction) that serves to help a Victim relieve the "pain" of Victimhood. As an activity, the Rescuer helps the Victim "numb out." Despite having helpful intentions, the Rescuer as a person reinforces the Victim's "Poor Me" by adopting a "Poor You" attitude, which serves to increase the Victim's sense of powerlessness. This renders the Victim dependent upon the Rescuer for a sense of safety—a bond forged by the Victim's shame for needing to be rescued and cemented by the Rescuer's own fear of abandonment or loss of purpose.

FISBE: This serves as the basis of the "mental model" that underpins the two Orientations. It is an acronym for the three elements of the model: where people put their Focus engages in them an emotional Inner State, which then drives their Behavior. The two primary mental models (Victim and Creator) are referred to as "Orientations" because what we focus on (i.e., *orient* on) has a great deal to do with what manifests in our experience.

Victim Orientation: It is in this Orientation that the DDT thrives. In this way of being, one's Focus is on the *problem* or *problems* that dominate one's life. When a problem occurs, it engages an inner state of *anxiety,* which in turn causes one to *react*. There are three basic forms of reacting: *fight, flight,* or *freeze.* The DDT is based on fear, avoidance (of feelings, loss, pain, reality), and/or aggressive reactivity. Much of humanity sleepwalks through life, unwittingly entangled in the DDT and the Victim Orientation in which it takes place. While the Victim Orientation has served a vital evolutionary purpose by helping humanity survive by reacting to threats in a hostile world, it has now outlived its usefulness as our "default" orientation.

Creator Orientation: The alternative to the Victim Orientation, this is the way of being in which The Empowerment Dynamic is cultivated. The FISBE here is much different. A Creator consciously focuses on a *vision* or *outcome*—that which she chooses to create in her life. As she focuses on what she wants to manifest, a Creator taps into an inner state of *passion*, which propels her to take a *Baby Step*. Each small movement is either an advancement toward the vision or a clarification of the final form of the desired outcome. A Creator still faces and solves problems, but she does so in the course of creating the outcomes, rather than merely reacting to them.

AIR: This acronym highlights the three key differences between the Victim and the Creator Orientation. The first is where you place your **A**ttention (on what's wanted instead of what's not wanted). The second is what you hold as your **I**ntention (manifesting outcomes, not just ridding yourself of problems). The third is **R**esults (satisfying and sustainable, not temporary and reactive). The acronym AIR also serves to reinforce the reality that a very different experience and environment (hence, "air") is generated by each of the two orientations.

Harnessing Dynamic Tension: Based on the work of Robert Fritz *(The Path of Least Resistance)*, Dynamic Tension is a way of planning for and taking action in creating outcomes. We begin by identifying and describing the *vision/outcome* we desire to create. The next step is to carefully and completely assess our *current reality* as it relates to the envisioned outcome. There are two aspects of the current situation that we identify. The first aspects are those things that are happening or exist that *support* and are helpful in the creation of the outcome. The second aspects are the problems, obstacles, or things that are missing that *inhibit* our capacity to manifest the vision. By focusing on both the outcome and the current reality, we engage the tension—a creative force —between what we want and where we are. This tension seeks to be resolved. A Creator resolves the tension by taking *Baby Steps* to move from current reality toward the desired outcome. Each small step brings learning—whether it results in a step "back," a step "forward," or a "quantum leap"—in the process of creating outcomes.

TED (*The Empowerment Dynamic): Creator, Challenger, Coach—*As a result of moving from the Victim Orientation to the Creator Orientation, a whole new set of roles and relationship dynamics becomes possible. The Empowerment Dynamic is made up of the following three roles, each of which serves as an antidote to the toxic roles of the DDT.

1. Creator. This is the central role of TED* and is the antidote to the powerless Victim. A Creator cultivates his capacity to create outcomes by adopting a Creator Orientation and harnessing Dynamic Tension. A Creator greatly increases his ability to choose a response to life circumstances (even in the harshest of situations), rather than merely reacting to them. Creators seek and form relationships with other Creators (Co-Creators), both to support and to be supported through the other two roles that make up TED*.

2. Challenger. Serving as an antidote to a Persecutor, who provokes a reaction from a Victim, a Challenger is a catalyst for change, learning, and growth for a Creator. A Challenger may be conscious and constructive, especially when in relationship with another Creator. Some of the Challengers we meet in life are unconscious—a person, condition, or circumstance that comes into our experience uninvited. In either case, a Creator is able to embrace the experience of a Challenger as a call to action, learning, and growth.

3. Coach. As the antidote to a Rescuer, who reinforces the powerlessness of a Victim, a Coach views others as being creative and resourceful. A Coach sees each person he relates to as a Creator in her own right, and seeks to support her in

the process of creating outcomes. A Coach does this by asking questions that help clarify envisioned outcomes, current realities, and possible Baby Steps. A Coach dares a Creator to dream and discern the pathways for manifesting her visions.

Shift Happens: Making "shift happen" from the Victim to the Creator Orientation and from the DDT roles to their antidotes in TED* is the pathway for transforming how we experience life and interact in relationships. The shift from Victim to Creator takes place by focusing on what we want rather than what we don't want, by moving from reacting to choosing outcomes and our responses to life experiences, and by reconnecting to our dreams and desires. Transforming our relationship with Persecutors so that we see them as Challengers instead calls upon us to discern the learning and growth they spark. To become a conscious Challenger in relationship with others requires clarity of intention, the ability to see the other as a Creator in his own right, and the wish to provoke and evoke growth and development. The shift from Rescuer to Coach invites us to see the other as creative and resourceful, and to support him in the creation process by asking questions and facilitating his own clarification of envisioned outcomes, the current realities he faces, and possible Baby Steps for moving forward.

Acknowledgments

for the 10th Anniversary edition

Many people have encouraged me and helped me bring TED* to you, and have contributed to the maturing of the book and body of work over the past decade. To those who have shared with me their heartfelt stories of how TED* has made a difference in their lives, I offer my heartfelt gratitude in return.

While there are many champions and promoters of TED*, I especially want to thank "early adopters" Bert Parlee, Ph.D.; Molly Gordon, MCC; Rand Stagen; and the incredible community of TED* Practitioners—those who have come forward and made TED* a part of their practice and service in the world. To the "Wizards" of Bainbridge Island: Jerilyn Drusseau, David Hager, Bob Linz, Carol Winkler, and Donna Zajonc, your encouragement and life-affirming support, feedback, and challenge have exemplified what an empowerment circle can be.

No one has influenced my thinking and my way of being in the world more than Bob Anderson, my decades-long friend and founder of The Leadership Circle, partner in the Full Circle Group and co-author of *Mastering Leadership*. Thanks for introducing me to the

Acknowledgments

Orientations and for encouraging me to find my own voice, my own ways of expressing them.

And to my dear fellow "Four Horsemen," Bob Anderson, Jim Anderson and Dan Holden and "Soul Sister," Barbara Braham, Ph.D.—as well as the circle of colleagues who have gathered around the tables at the University of Notre Dame while serving as coaches for the Executive Integral Leadership Program—a deep bow of gratitude for your love and support in facing my own "dark nights" of the DDT, while always affirming the Creator essence we all share.

The contributions of two special editors and publishing consultants cannot be overstated. Ceci Miller, as the original editor and publishing coach, thanks for the challenge to develop the story that became TED*, and for coaching and coaxing the various voices of the story into being. You were a wonderful midwife (and thanks for introducing me to Roy!). Roy M. Carlisle, you expertly shepherded the second edition that grew TED* to maturity and made it accessible to an even wider circle of readers. This 10th Anniversary edition may never have come to fruition without your encouragement, persistence, publisher and bookseller sensibilities.

Acknowledgments

And to Donna—wife and partner extraordinaire—the word gratitude pales in comparison to what my heart and head really want to say about the contribution you bring to my life and our work. For your early admonition to write down the shift from the Drama Triangle to what you helped me name as The Empowerment Dynamic, for the magical suggestions that came out of our innumerable morning "quiet time" meditations, for reading every single word of the manuscript, and for constantly cheering me on, I thank you with all my heart. You have been an incredible companion every step of the way. You are, indeed, "TED*'s mom."

Suggested Reading and References

The following books, articles, and resources directly influenced the writing of this book. For additional resources, please visit *www.PowerofTED.com.*

Allen, James. *As a Man Thinketh.* Forth Worth, TX: Brownlow Publishing, 1985.

Chopra, Deepak. *The Seven Spiritual Laws of Success: A Practical Guide to the Fulfillment of Your Dreams.* San Rafael, CA: Amber-Allen Publishing and New World Library, 1994.

Frankl, Viktor E. *Man's Search for Meaning.* New York: Washington Square Press, 1984.

Fritz, Robert. *The Path of Least Resistance: Learning to Become the Creative Force in Your Own Life.* New York: Fawcett Columbine, 1989.

Nouwen, Henri. *Bread for the Journey: A Daybook of Wisdom and Faith.* New York: HarperCollins, 1997.

Rilke, Rainer Maria. *Letters to a Young Poet.* Translated by M. D. Herter Norton. Revised Edition. New York: Norton & Company, Inc., 1993.

A number of references to Stephen Karpman and The Drama Triangle are available on the Internet. The following three were particularly helpful in the writing of this book:

Forest, Lynne. *The Three Faces of Victim.* http://www.lynneforrest.com/html/the_faces_of_victim.html

Karpman, Steve, with comments by Patty E. Fleener M.S.W. 2002-2004. *The Drama Triangle.* http://www.mental-health-today.com/articles/drama.htm

Namka, Lynne, Ed.D. 2004. *The Drama Triangle: Three Faces of Victimhood.* http://www.angriesout.com/grown20.htm

For more information on Stephen Karpman and the Drama Triangle, visit his website: www.KarpmanDramaTriangle.com.

INDEX

Index

Index

Index

ABOUT DAVID EMERALD

David Emerald is a confirmed Creator who once viewed life through the eyes of a Victim. He makes his home on a peaceful island in the Pacific Northwest in the United States, where he likes to walk the beach and imagine the best of all possible futures.

David Emerald is also the pen name of David Emerald Womeldorff, cofounder of the Bainbridge Leadership Center, along with his wife, Donna Zajonc. It offers a wide range of products and services in three interdependent areas of practice: public leadership, organizational leadership, and self-leadership.

The Power of TED* serves as a focal point for self-leadership. David has drawn on decades of communication, leadership, and organization development experience in writing this fable on self-leadership out of his conviction that how one leads one's own life is highly correlated to the quality of one's leadership as a whole.

For more information, visit **www.PowerofTED.com**.